Praise for
Moms Moving On

"If you're going through a divorce and have young children, get your hands on this book! I know from personal and professional experience that it's essential to have the right guide during the traumatic time of divorce. Michelle Dempsey-Multack provides an honest, funny, and deeply real look at the struggles and triumphs of going through a divorce. She covers all the sticky areas no one else wants to talk about, highlights helpful strategies to manage difficult situations, and tells you who to reach out to when you need help. . . . *Moms Moving On* is a gift to all moms who are making the brave choice to move past their marriages."

—Dr. Elizabeth Cohen, "Divorce Doctor"
and author of *Light on the Other Side of Divorce*

"This book is what every mother who's either contemplating divorce, presently going through divorce, or dealing with life after divorce needs to read in order to feel more empowered and secure as a parent and as a woman, particularly during a time that tends to challenge one's confidence and self-assurance. Michelle's authenticity and relatability is trustworthy and will leave mothers feeling like they're speaking to a best friend who just happens to be an expert in the field. This book can be an incredible resource to help mothers transition from 'surviving' mode to 'thriving' mode!"

—Evelyn Mendal, LMHC and early childhood expert

"Michelle Dempsey-Multack has a gift for taking the deeply emotional and personal experience of divorce, both as a child of a high-conflict divorce and as a mother navigating the choppy waters of the process herself, and making it accessible to those who need support the most. In *Moms Moving On*, Michelle's advice, sharing of relatable experiences, and tell-it-like-it-is words of wisdom provide a wealth of support and understanding at a time when many feel so alone. This is the book that will help you survive, thrive, and move on!"

—Susan Guthrie, leading family law attorney, mediator, and award-winning host of *The Divorce & Beyond Podcast*

"Nobody supports co-parenting and divorced moms like Michelle Dempsey-Multack. Whether you're currently going through it or you've already been through it and just need a reminder that you're not alone, Michelle will lift you up and empower you to make the best choices for yourself and your children. We can do hard things, especially with someone like Michelle in our corner."

—Samantha Angoletta, executive editor at Scary Mommy

MOMS MOVING ON

MOMS MOVING ON

REAL-LIFE ADVICE *on* CONQUERING DIVORCE, CO-PARENTING THROUGH CONFLICT, *and* BECOMING YOUR BEST SELF

MICHELLE DEMPSEY-MULTACK, MS, CDS

SIMON ELEMENT

New York   London   Toronto   Sydney   New Delhi

SIMON ELEMENT

An Imprint of Simon & Schuster, Inc.

1230 Avenue of the Americas

New York, NY 10020

First Simon Element trade paperback edition March 2023

SIMON ELEMENT is a trademark of Simon & Schuster, Inc.

For information about special discounts for bulk purchases, please contact Simon & Schuster Special Sales at 1-866-506-1949 or business@simonandschuster.com.

The Simon & Schuster Speakers Bureau can bring authors to your live event. For more information or to book an event, contact the Simon & Schuster Speakers Bureau at 1-866-248-3049 or visit our website at www.simonspeakers.com.

Interior design by Davina Mock-Maniscalco

Manufactured in the United States of America

10 9 8 7 6 5 4 3 2 1

The Library of Congress has cataloged the hardcover edition as follows:

Names: Dempsey-Multack, Michelle, author.
Title: Moms moving on : real life advice for conquering divorce, co-parenting
    through conflict, and becoming your best self / by Michelle Dempsey-Multack
    MS, CDS.
Description: First Tiller Press hardcover edition. | New York : Tiller Press, 2022. |
    Includes bibliographical references.
Identifiers: LCCN 2021030955 (print) | LCCN 2021030956 (ebook) |
    ISBN 9781982184582 (hardcover) | ISBN 9781982184599 (ebook)
Subjects: LCSH: Divorced mothers. | Divorced people—Family relationships.
Classification: LCC HQ814 .D39 2022 (print) | LCC HQ814 (ebook) |
    DDC 306.89/3—dc23
LC record available at https://lccn.loc.gov/2021030955
LC ebook record available at https://lccn.loc.gov/2021030956

ISBN 978-1-9821-8458-2
ISBN 978-1-9821-8460-5 (pbk)
ISBN 978-1-9821-8459-9 (ebook)

To Mom, Bella, Nanny, and Spencer.
The one who taught me to fly, the one who inspires me to fly,
the one who encourages my flight, and the one who flies with me.
I love you to the moon.

Contents

MOMS MOVING ON

A Few Things Before
We Begin . . .

Please know that the words I've put on these pages only became clear to me after years of falling on my face and learning things the hard way. I had to go through it all myself before I could share the lessons with you, in the hope that they might help you move on too. Please know that however dark it may seem in the midst of divorce, you are strong, deserving of all good things, and have all the courage and fortitude you need to make it through this part of your life. And if you don't yet know how to harness that courage and fortitude, or you need a little reminder of just how badass you can be, you've come to the right place. This is moving on, Mama, and I'm here to help. I'm a divorced mom, divorce coach, and Certified Divorce Specialist. I have a background in journalism and education, which fueled my desire to teach other women through my writing and speaking career. I separated from my daughter's father when she was just two years old (not something I wished for but definitely something I've learned and grown from) and have been co-parenting for almost five years now. I'm also a child of divorce, who has made it her mission to do this divorce and co-parenting thing as well-informed and as positively as possible. My mission in life is to give women the kind of support, knowledge, and empowerment that they deserve during divorce, and I'm grateful to have that opportunity every single day of my life.

One of my favorite tools, which I hope you'll also try as you read this book, is journaling. I firmly believe that no one realizes how powerful it can be to write down their thoughts until they've been through some shit. Not a single client I work with escapes my obsession with journaling. As Ernest Hemingway once said, "There is nothing to writing. All you do is sit down at a typewriter and bleed."

I'll be giving journal prompts at the end of every chapter. Don't be intimidated—embrace it! Invest in a journal that feels good to hold, that's nice to look at. Hell, go for the one with the cheesy inspirational "You go, girl!" quote on the front. Do yourself a favor and give it a try.

A quick disclaimer: Of course, all divorcing couples face the same pain and problems. Some aspects of this book, because it's so deeply informed by my own experience, are written from a heterosexual perspective, but I truly believe that the tools and tips therein will be useful to anyone in this situation. But I'm always looking to learn more about the full range of divorce experiences, so if you're going through it and you don't see yourself represented in these pages, I want to know! DM me @themichelledempsey.

It's Over

As my ex carried his last box of stuff out of our house, I did what any scorned woman would do: I ripped our framed wedding vows off the bedroom wall, smashed the frame to bits, and tore up his beautiful, heartfelt, handwritten vows in the most dramatic way possible. I chased him out the door like some possessed bat-out-of-hell crazy woman, before getting mad at myself for making a huge mess in my bedroom. As I picked up all of the broken little pieces of a life once lived, I prayed to God my toddler wouldn't end up stepping on a hidden shard of glass. Turning my Oscar-worthy performance of "our marriage is over" into a trip to the ER was not something I could handle at that moment.

I was still on all fours in front of my bedroom mirror when I caught a glimpse of myself and heard a voice inside me say, "What the hell are you so angry about? You didn't have the right marriage for you. You knew this couldn't continue. *Stop.*"

Right then and there, I decided that I wasn't going to make this divorce about loss. I wasn't going to sit around crying over him anymore—I had done that enough already in our last three years of being together. I spent more time crying myself to sleep, crying in the shower, and crying in the car after fights—more than any woman should have cried. I cried for the way I couldn't make this work between us. I cried for the fact that each of my flaws and shortcomings, undealt-with traumas, and fears came to the surface at every turn in this marriage. I cried for the fact that my marriage wouldn't fix me. At this point, I was all cried out and then some.

If I was going to cry any more, it was going to be out of frustration and discomfort, not over the relationship that had just imploded. I was getting divorced. That was the new hard truth to accept. I was no longer fighting for a marriage to work; I was about to start fighting for it to come undone.

I wasn't dying, losing a limb, or struggling with a life-threatening illness. I was getting divorced. There's a huge difference.

And that's exactly what you need to realize. This book is designed to help you get through it, get beyond it, and become your best self. I wasn't my best self at that moment, for sure, but I put in the work over years to pick myself up, dust myself off, and move on.

What comes next in these pages is a lot of honesty, love, advice, reassurance, and things you can act on right now to help you move on after your divorce.

I've been there. I know what it's like—all of it.

Let's move on.

CHAPTER 1

Pulling Yourself Out of Bed
After Reality Sets In

MOMMMYYYYYYYYY," you hear as you're jolted awake, far too early as usual. Is it Tuesday? Sunday? Did this all really just happen? Are you really there alone, waking up in an existence you never hoped for? You lie there silently, hoping the whining will stop and you can bury your head back into the cool comfort of your new pillows—the ones you bought as you stripped your mattress of its old "married" bedding. The mommy call comes again, only this time louder and more persistent. You wish you could just nudge the guy next to you and promise you'll get up with the kids tomorrow—but, oh yeah, there's no one there.

You know you have no choice but to pull your emotionally exhausted body out of bed, but you can't, *you just can't*. Because as your eyes open, the reminder blares through your head like a tornado siren, announcing its presence in the distance. The reality of where you've somehow landed flushes your cheeks and sends a tingle through your hands and feet. *I'm getting divorced,* you remember, as your child continues crying out for you.

How the hell am I going to do this? you ask yourself. *How is it even possible to carry on, take care of these kids, weather the divorce storm, and maintain some semblance of normalcy in my life? Maybe I can't. Maybe if I just stay here, it will all go away.*

The thought of it not going away is damn near paralyzing. Lying in bed with the covers pulled up to your chin from now until forever sounds like a great plan, but there are kids that need to be fed, driven to school, clothed, and cared for. You really have no choice but to get up and face what's out there. It's a heavy burden.

MY FIRST FORTY-EIGHT HOURS

"Where should we go for dinner tonight?" I asked my brother, just hours after the door slammed behind my ex for the last time.

"Michelle, you just got separated this morning," he replied with shock. "Why don't you take it easy tonight?"

"Why would we take it easy?" I shouted back. "I have to eat. You have to eat. You're only in town for a few more days and I'm not going to just sit at home because my marriage ended. I'm not going to be one of those sad, divorced, woe-is-me kinda gals. No way. What's for dinner?"

"We're ordering in," he insisted, as my best friend texted that she was on her way with wine.

I called my mom in a tizzy. "Mom, you better tell your son that I don't need a pity party. I don't understand what the problem is! Why does he treat me like I'm some kind of crazy person for wanting to go out to dinner?"

Having been through an epic, showstopping, nine-and-a-half-year divorce herself, my mom knew I was still in denial. She knew that even though this split was a long time in the making and I would, indeed, end up okay, the reality hadn't set in yet. I was riding a wave of adrenaline coupled with some forcibly sum-moned self-confidence, determined to act as if everything was fine so that I, too, could believe it.

"Honey, just take it easy," she pleaded. "Your whole life just changed." She was packing for a trip out of the country, which, in my mind, wouldn't have been part of her plans if she didn't honestly believe I was going to be okay on my own. I thought she was being completely unreasonable. Hadn't she heard me say that I was perfectly fine?

The morning after my split, my daughter was slated to go to a second-birthday party that would be attended by all our clos-est friends. I woke up early, curled my hair, and blasted some Beyoncé through the house as Bella and I got ready for yet an-other Minnie Mouse–themed gymnastics party. *I don't need a husband to accompany me to a birthday party*, I told myself, completely forgetting I'd be walking alone into a room full of "marrieds." Rumblings of gossip about my impending divorce had already begun circulating through my community. I can still remember the way my friends looked at me as I waltzed in, carrying Bella with one arm and a giant, perfectly wrapped gift with the other. I was the lion in the cage, and they were the eager onlookers at the zoo, waiting to see what kind of drama would ensue.

Then, someone threw a piece of raw meat into the cage.

"Hey, where's your better half?" my friend's husband asked jokingly as my friend nudged his side. "Football's over. I thought he'd be here!"

"Nope," I said, tossing my blown-out hair as if I didn't have a care in the world. "He couldn't be here—we split up yesterday." I made my way to the coffee table, working my hardest to deflect from the obvious and pretend everything was A-okay.

Jaws hit the floor—and that, my friends, is how you turn the cake-cutting at a sweet little girl's second birthday party into a really awkward moment.

I went home that day more than convinced that I had somehow escaped the pain and angst and anger I'd always heard about. I also wondered how long everyone at that party would be spending on the phone that night debriefing from my post-divorce birthday parade, but that was an entirely different issue that I didn't have time for.

I had told myself, for years before the actual split, that I was built for this. I had lived divorce my entire life—my folks had the ugliest kind imaginable. Yet I watched my mom rise from the ashes like a phoenix and then move on with grace and elegance. I was going to prosper, persevere, and push forward just like her, proving that you don't need to be married to live your best life.

Then, the very next day, the weight came crashing down when Bella and I both woke up with the flu. I lay in bed, paralyzed by the sheer reality of being alone and the scale of my responsibilities. Bella's fever, and mine, slowly crept higher, but I couldn't yell for anyone to bring a box of tissues up the stairs or help me clean up the vomit from the carpet, vomit that just didn't seem to stop coming.

This is exactly the kind of shit that no one warns you about.

PUKE-STAINED CARPETS

Yup, just like that, I went from *Yeah, baby, I've GOT this* to cleaning up toddler puke on my hands and knees, with no lifeline to call on for help. My mom was gone and wouldn't be back for weeks. To this day, I remember the agony of having to spend $32 on Instacart for some stranger to bring Pedialyte to my doorstep within a two-hour window, because I had no one else to run the errand for me.

And it sucked. But you already know this process sucks. You know that when a marriage comes crashing down, life changes in an instant—literally—whether you like it or not.

So, what now? What next? Do you lie in bed all day and stare at the ceiling fan, hoping that if you watch its rapid spin for long enough, you'll be lulled into a hypnotic trance so deep that all your worries disappear?

Please don't do that.

Don't get me wrong. You need to grieve. You need to cry, and you need to feel, and you need to exorcise the demons of the relationship that did you wrong—there's no getting around that.

But you also need to learn there's a time and place for that grieving. When you're in your shower, after putting the kids to bed. In your car when that damn song comes on again. In bed, on a Saturday night when you're alone for the first time in years. But you can't wallow in it. You cannot let the quicksand of your emotions pull you under and keep you there, because the longer you stay under the weight of your pain, the harder it is to crawl out.

And if you feel tempted to tell yourself a story that isn't true—that you can't possibly understand how you got here—don't play that game. You know exactly how you got here; you just didn't want to have to take this road.

But you had to, because something was broken. Out of order. And now you're here. With kids to take care of, money to earn, and a whole host of adult responsibilities to sort out. Maybe you've heard the old saying, that it takes half the time you were with someone to truly get over them and move on. Let's say you were married for six years. That would mean you'd be spending the next 1,095 days crying over your ex. Is that what you want?

NO THANK YOU, YOU HAVE THINGS TO DO.

And frankly, why give in to the temptation to wallow when there are ways to move on more quickly—and maybe even gain some strength in the process?

There's a whole life waiting for you that looks a hell of a lot different from your old one, and that's not necessarily a bad thing.

So, now, you're going to put one foot in front of the other, just like you have always done before. You're going to think back to all the trials that life has brought you thus far—the ones that seemed damn near impossible to get through—and remind yourself that you did, indeed, get through them.

Now: some practical ideas about how to get out of that bed.

CREATE A PLAN YOU CAN STICK TO

There's a lot on your mind right now, understandably. This is a big reason for the sense of dread you wake up with every morning. It's also probably why you're having such a hard time moving on. You're scared of all that the future may hold for you, as a single mom.

Here's a great way to conquer those fears, a solution to all those big problems that feel so much bigger than they really are: Take a few hours, or a whole day even, to sit down and make a list of all the things that you'll need to tackle in the next few months. Let yourself see it on paper, to realize that your new responsibilities aren't as scary or un-deal-with-able as they seem. Create a timeline to put your mind at ease. For example:

By the end of this month, I will:

✦ Finally get the leaky faucet fixed that my ex kept putting off

✦ Look into more affordable car insurance options

✦ Get a bikini wax because I've completely neglected my nether regions while tending to everyone else

By the end of the summer, I will:

✦ Sit down with a financial planner

✦ Pay off that damn Nordstrom bill

✦ Meet with a few divorce attorneys to find the one that I feel most comfortable hiring

I'm telling you, there's magic to getting all of your worries out on paper instead of letting them run around in that hamster wheel of a brain you've got going on right now.

START A JOURNALING PRACTICE

Speaking of paper: congratulations, you've just become a writer!

Every morning when you wake up, before the relentless calls of your children start reverberating through the house, grab a pen and get to work in your journal.

Write about your feelings, your worries, your hopes, your dreams.

Write until you feel like the last of your sorrows or stresses or silly little thoughts have left your body for the time being.

Feeling down? Write about it.

Feeling more emotional than ever? Write about it.

Want to run your ex-husband, ex-boss, or soon-to-be-ex-mother-in-law over with a truck? Write about it.

Some days you won't have more than a sentence to write, and other days the kids might be running late for school because you had a really good flow going.

Afraid you won't know what to write about? Don't worry. Here are a few journal prompts to help you get started:

1. List ten words your best friends would use to describe you.

2. Describe the last time you felt truly desirable or powerful. What made you feel that way?

3. List all the reasons why your ex sucks.

4. Think of all the personality traits you'd want your partner to celebrate.

5. Think of how you want your kids to describe you when they're older.

6. Ask yourself whether you miss the person or miss what you thought you had.

Journaling is, in fact, therapeutic—which makes me thankful all the time that writing about my life is what I do for a living. In an Australian study published by *Psychology Today*, it was reported that the simple act of putting pen to paper serves as an escape—the kind that every mama dealing with the pain of divorce can certainly benefit from.[1] What's more, if you're feeling especially angry, hurt, sad, or all of the above, you can make journaling more physical for an added dose of stress relief. Journaling, or "expressive writing," as they called it, "led to reduced blood pressure, improved immune system functioning, fewer visits to the doctor and shorter stays in the hospital, improved mood, reduced symptoms of depression, improved memory, and more." The same study also found that expressive writing "helped people to confront emotions they were avoiding and cognitively process what's happened to them. There's also some evidence that revisiting difficult emotions in a controlled way can help people move past those emotions."

This is why I love journaling. It's like the elevated mama's way of letting out all of that negative energy without having to slash her soon-to-be-ex's tires.

Journaling is my tried-and-true way of being able to pull myself out of bed feeling like I've done my share of worrying and reflecting for the day. Try it. I bet it will do the same for you.

FIND WHAT MAKES YOU TINGLE

Often, when I'm working with a new client, she'll tell me that she feels she lost herself in the marriage, and just wants to find herself again. I'll ask what her "thing" is, the thing that still makes her tingle, or the hobby that she's cultivated over the years. Then she'll scoff and say something like, "Well, I loved painting, it was such a release for me, but my husband always complained that I made a mess with all of the paint colors in the garage."

Well, fuck him and the colorless horse he rode in on. It's time to paint! Or cook. Or sit on the couch for a solid hour each day—pants off, hair up, book in hand.

Whatever it is, harness the thing. Hold tight to it and make it a point to do this thing every single day. Or every couple of days, since you're a mom, and who has that much extra time?

The point is, connecting your new marital status to something you love doing helps reframe the whole *What the hell am I supposed to do now?* argument that's been running through your head. It gives you a sense of purpose, something to look forward to, and takes you out of that "I'm just a single mom with no time for myself" mindset. Make a date with your thing whenever possible, and let it motivate you to get the hell out of bed.

STICK A NOTE ON YOUR BATHROOM MIRROR

Toward the end of my marriage, before I decided to divorce, I was feeling lost, hopeless, and desperate for some relief and direction. I took a friend's advice and visited an energy healer. Now, if you knew me, you'd know that I'm typically more likely to scoff at the idea of someone being able to heal my energy than beg for their phone number (which is what I did), but desperate times call for desperate measures. Such as driving almost two hours to a complete stranger's home, lying down on a table in her living room with my eyes closed, and letting her burn things and bang rocks together all around my body.

It was a cloudy day in the middle of the week, the kind you get in south Florida when everything feels heavy because of the contrast with the mostly warm, sunny days. The weight of my marriage coupled with this seasonal shift made it feel as if I'd trudged through quicksand to this woman's door. Her home smelled of patchouli and other varieties of incense. The walls were painted a striking emerald green, and the furniture was covered in floral patterns and hints of gold.

Then, to my surprise, the healing began. She was fucking fabulous. Something she did during that session—I'm still not sure what—really awoke something inside me and helped me get clear on where I was headed, and what I needed to do to get there. Before I left her home that day, she handed me a pad of paper and a Sharpie and asked me to write myself a note full of intentions. I was supposed to write what I envisioned for my future, what I wanted the universe to bring me, and to stick it on my bathroom mirror to greet me every morning.

At the time, this sounded crazier than driving to her house in the first place, but I thought, *screw it.* I had already thrown my hat in the ring, so I might as well play.

At this point in my life, things were going really well in my career, and I wanted to keep that momentum going. I also knew deep in my heart that while this marriage was just seconds away from imploding, there was a great love out there waiting for me, because I wasn't done with love yet.

This is what I wrote, as this random woman and all her crystals watched over me:

Dear Michelle,

You are so inspirational and empowering; women everywhere can't get enough of hearing you speak and reading your articles. You're going to keep uplifting others with your strength while raising your daughter to be the very best she can be. Your book will be a NYT bestseller and you'll sell out conferences and workshops around the world. You'll fall so deeply in love with yourself, and then with someone who deserves you and respects the hell out of you. Keep going, you beautiful, badass woman!

I took this letter home and taped it to the bathroom mirror and read it multiple times a day, each time believing more and more in the words I had written. After every read, I found myself breathless at the fact that these words had poured out of me in a matter of seconds, as if my soul knew exactly what it needed but had never been asked.

I'd like you to write yourself a note now, too, even if you think it's silly. It always ends up being my clients' favorite assignment. What do you want most in the world? How are you going to get it?

HAVE A GOOD CRY

If you feel like crying, do it—give yourself some time alone and let it all out. My clients often start to cry and then say, "Oh my god I'm so sorry, I don't know why I'm crying. I feel so stupid!"

Why? For having well-functioning tear ducts and natural human emotions? Don't be silly. No one is expecting you to have it all together. The real power comes from knowing that even when you do cry, when the whole damn divorce bowl of lemons seems sour and hopeless, you know how to make tomorrow a better day.

You deserve that. Your kids deserve that. Your future deserves that.

Note that earlier, I spoke about trying not to fall apart in front of your children. That's the one exception to crying whenever and wherever you want. The adults in your life— friends, family, coworkers, bosses, hairstylists, trainers—can handle your tears. Your kids shouldn't have to. That being said, it might happen. You might cry in front of your kids. If you do, own it. Say, "I'm just sad right now and crying helps. I'll be okay." It's good for them to know that tears are nothing to be ashamed of.

LONG STORY SHORT

✦ This is tough stuff; don't pretend that it's not. Crying is okay. It's necessary. It's healing.

✦ Luckily, you have a really strong "why" when it comes to getting out of bed: your kids.

✦ Get prepared, and plan ahead to quiet your anxiety.

✦ Get clear on one thing that you love doing and make time for it as often as possible.

✦ Write your bathroom mirror note.

✦ Breathe. There's a whole lot of stuff coming down the pipeline.

✦ Breathe. You've got this.

JOURNAL PROMPT

List your favorite ways to quiet your anxiety.

The Five W's of Breaking the News (Who, What, When, Where, Why, and How to Spill the Divorce Beans)

I'm so sorry to hear about your divorce," my mom's well-intentioned friend blurted out, a few weeks after my split. We were standing in line at my neighborhood coffee shop. You know the one: where everyone knows your name and every table is filled with women gossiping about the town's latest split, affair, or who cut them off in the school carpool line.

I felt the pulse of the room start to slow as mine quickened. The blood rushed to my cheeks, and my hands started to tingle. *Good news travels fast*, I thought as I did an internal eye-roll. I could feel my mom tense up and hold her breath, terrified of what might come out of my mouth. She had already asked me to at least *pretend* I was sad when people would offer their "condolences." Her fingers were already on the back of my arm, ready to squeeze if I dared embarrass her.

The thing was, though, I wasn't feeling sad—at least, not

in the way this woman was implying—and I wasn't about to pretend I was. So, how to handle the giant box of pity she was waiting to unpack? I wasn't ashamed of the news—quite the opposite, in fact. I was proud. Proud of the idea that I took my life into my own hands and made the gut-wrenching decision to turn it upside down and start over. Proud that I could face the world with the scarlet *D* emblazoned on my Lululemon sports bra *and* still smile. Frankly, I would have put it on the back of a denim jacket as I paraded around town, if I could have.

I mean, yeah, I get it, a marriage was over. There was a fantastic wedding. What a band! Oh, and that cocktail hour! Did you see her shoes? Were they Valentino? There was money spent, weight lost, hours spent agonizing over flowers, linens, and music. There were beautiful vows exchanged. We meant those words, I know we did, because we loved each other.

But sometimes love just isn't enough. Sometimes it gets lost. The end of a marriage is a kind of loss.

But it's also a time of renewal and hope and possibility. The woman in the coffee shop didn't know what had happened in my marriage. She had no idea that there was, in fact, nothing to pity me for.

And here's the thing: I owed her nothing—no information, no story, no fake reaction. She was not my problem. *I needed an almond milk latte, extra hot, and then I needed to get the hell out of there.*

The second you decide to get divorced, you're going to have to deal with other people. The first thing to do is make a plan for who to tell what, when, and how. That's what this chapter is all about.

You may have already experienced a coffee shop moment

like this. It ain't fun. It's disappointing, really, in its predictability. But there *are* ways to handle it.

First, accept that your split is the equivalent of Moses parting the Red Sea, or the fifty-yard line on a football field. An invisible line suddenly appears, cleanly dividing the people in your life. There are two groups now—the Flockers and the Fleers—and identifying them is a skill you need to master.

The what?

THE FLOCKERS AND THE FLEERS

Let's start with the ones who flee, because they, in some ways, are easier to deal with. One half of the people you'd call your friends, acquaintances, or favorite coworkers become the fleers. Like wildlife heading for the highest point of ground before the tsunami hits, these people want nothing—I mean *nothing*—to do with the fact that you're getting divorced. It scares them, paralyzes them with the idea that they, too, could end up in your shoes. Before you know it, they've stopped asking to make plans, let texts go unanswered, and stammer awkwardly when they run into you at Target.

These are the same people who don't laugh when someone trips, and who have the strength to look away when passing a nasty car wreck. At first, this is going to feel really hurtful for you. I get it, because I experienced this mass exodus of connections virtually as soon as the word got out. I didn't understand it then, but I do now. It's one of those "it's not you, it's me" things, and it's almost better that they're giving you your space to deal with the Flockers, because that's who will demand most of your energy.

Your Real Problem: The Flockers

The Flockers are the opposite of the Fleers. They're the ones who not only slow down their car to crane their necks and soak in every detail of that car wreck on the side of the road, but also whip out their phones, snap some photos, and post them on social media without the slightest bit of shame. They ask why you had your car accident. ("Why couldn't you have swerved out of the way? Didn't you see the boulder in the road? Well, what are you going to do now? Get another car, I hope!")

These Flockers may mean well, but when they start in with their pity and their questions, all you'll want to do is scream, "WELL, THEN GO AND MARRY HIM YOURSELF, WHY DON'T YA?"

The problem is, much like my mom's friend in the coffee shop, these Flockers don't know the half of your story, and what led you to where you are right now.

That woman didn't know that there were years upon years of shit I had to wade through in order to even gather the strength to split from my husband.

She didn't know that this pain came from being the product of a home ripped apart, a single mother who stopped at nothing to move her life forward, onward, and upward.

She didn't know that just three years ago, my self-esteem was nonexistent, and I was nothing more than a hologram of myself: perfectly fine on the outside but vapid, blurry, and utterly confused on the inside.

She didn't know that giving birth to my daughter finally helped me make sense of it all, that all my pain had finally come to a head, and that I was no longer going to soak in it, using it as an excuse for my failures. She didn't know that having a child was when I finally *found myself* in my marriage, coming to terms with all my mistakes and flaws.

She didn't know that it takes two to get divorced, and that the end of a marriage is often the result of two who failed, not one.

She didn't know the half of it—and I wasn't about to tell her.

Your Flockers aren't going to know all that about you either, about the particular circumstances that led you to this point. I can offer you some ideas about how to handle them, but before we launch an all-out midnight witch hunt on the Flockers, I want to remind you of a hard truth here: You, too, have stood in the Flockers' shoes. At one time or another, you *have* been tossed the gossip ball from a friend and run straight to another friend to let her score another touchdown. You have questioned someone else's reality with your own perspective. We all have. It's called being human. It's desperately trying to find truth in someone else's story, while escaping from our own lives for just a little bit. And of course, it's a way to ward off our own misfortune, however misguidedly.

Now that you know the landscape of Flock vs. Flee, let me give you some insight into all those post-divorce questions coming your way.

Who Are the Flockers?

Your Flockers are going to include a wide range of interesting characters. Prepare for everyone from your grandmother, her favorite canasta buddy, your mom's friend at the coffee shop, and the lovely employee at your dry cleaner to *every single other person* in your family and friend group who fits the Flocker frame. Pepper in a few acquaintances around town who have "heard the sad news," and you have yourself a well-rounded cacophony of lookie-loos who *must* know what went down behind the scenes in your marriage, and they'll want to know NOW.

What fuels their motivation? Simple: fear. They're not out searching for information on your split because they want to hurt you. More often than not, people—or women, rather—go on this deep dive for details in hope that knowing every last ugly truth can help them avoid the same fate. You have to accept that people want to understand your situation as some kind of subconscious defense mechanism.

WHEN WILL THE FLOODGATES OPEN?

The questions will start flooding in as soon as you break the seal on your new divorce truth. You'll wonder if an ad was taken out in the local newspaper, or someone flew a banner behind a small prop plane over the beach on a holiday weekend. Brace yourself, Mama; take a few deep breaths. The questions will come, and then they will go. You, the end of your marriage, and what you intend to do about it will not be the topic on everyone's minds for the rest of eternity. They'll all get over it as soon as someone else's gossip hits the airwaves.

WHAT DO THEY WANT TO KNOW?

Well, this is obvious, because we all know what they want to know. They want to know why this lovely union is no more, and I'll get to the reasons why you should be discerning about your story, below. But very few Flockers are going to come right out and ask. They're going to ask it in a way that takes the edge off the ol' "So, why'd you get divorced?" and wrap it in a neat and tidy bow instead.

Here's what those little gifts will sound like:

Them: "But he was such a nice boy!"

You're most likely going to hear this from your grandma, your great-aunt, and some of your nosiest neighbors.

Here's how I've answered this: "Still is, but I'm well overdue for a nice *man*." Or, "Well, he's back on the market now; shall I give you his phone number?" Or, better yet, "Nice does not a marriage make."

Them: "Seriously? You guys looked sooooooo happy!"

This will come from your social media contacts whom you don't actually speak to in real life. You know, the ones who assume they know you based solely off what you post.

Here's how I've rebutted this ridiculous assumption:

"Did you post your last knock-down, drag-out fight with your husband on social media? Yeah, me neither." Or, "Don't judge a book by its highlight reel."

Them: "Oh my god, but didn't you want to make it work for the kids?"

This seemingly judgy, passive-aggressive question is going to come from just about anyone who is a.) completely uneducated about the disservice two unhappily married people do to their kids, or b.) the people in your life with young kids who may be unhappily married and are seeking validation themselves.

This is one I could never just pass off with a sarcastic quip. This one always threw gas on the fire within me, waking up my need to set the record straight. Whenever I heard this, I'd immediately think of my mother, who, as an immigrant with barely any support system in the United States, left a cheating man to set a good example for her kids. She, like me, believed you don't fight for someone who will hurt you, because that's not a good lesson to teach young children.

The hard truth on this one: your kids deserve a happy mom, not a married one. Plain and simple. Your kids will benefit much more from being raised by a thriving single mother than in a home filled with tension driven by two unhappily married people. One of the most comforting articles I read on this topic while doing research for an article back in 2019, "Should You Stay Together Only for the Kids?" came from *Psychology Today*, and told me everything I needed to know about the reality of staying married just for the kids:[1]

> In the long term . . . divorce can lead to happier outcomes for children. When parents are arguing or incompatible in a deep and lasting way, divorce can be a relief for children, a chance to breathe healthier air, free of the tensions of an unhappy relationship. When changes in family structure are handled well, children experience a temporary disruption but can achieve long-term resiliency and strength.
>
> If you are thinking about your children's ability to create happily productive adult lives for themselves, then, the answer [to whether or not you should just stay married] is no. Try your best to make your marriage work, but don't stay in an unhappy relationship only for the sake of your children.

The simple answer to give people who ask this question is: "It's far more important to me that my child witness happiness than toxicity."

Them: "Aw, I'm sure there's a way you two can work it out. Divorce is awful—you don't want to go through that!"

Another knee slapper from the cheap seats in the back. This is what I call the "Back to the Future" question, because this comment almost always begs the response of, "So, should I just hop back in my time machine and erase all of the mistrust, pain, anger, and already-filed divorce papers, or what?" This is almost always a projection from someone whose worst fear would be to end up where you are right now.

Here's how I've responded to this: "If we could have worked it out, we would have, and to be honest, I feel much better now than I have in years, so, divorce really isn't that awful for me, thanks!"

Them: "Welcome to the club, Mama. I'm SO happy for you."

This. *This.* THIS is the kind of energy you need in your new post-divorce life, and you will almost always get it from other divorced women. This kind of encouragement can only come from the women who have been there, lived it, and grown from it. Seek these ladies out, because they're critically important to your new divorce journey. Where can you find them? Almost all divorce coaches, much like myself, will have a Facebook group or other online community for you to join. This is ideal for the mom who doesn't yet have any other divorced friends in her community, and will help you feel so understood, so un-lonely, and so supported.

WHY BE DISCERNING ABOUT
WHAT YOU TELL PEOPLE?

Well, I know times are tough right now and your vulnerability cup runneth over, but I want you to think about this "why" question long and hard. You want people to know the truth; I know you do. I wanted people to know *my* truth; I would have screamed it from the rooftops if I could have. But I couldn't have. You know why? It all boils down to respect: respect for my daughter, Bella, and yes, respect for the man who was no longer my husband but would remain a presence in Bella's life for years to come.

Protecting my daughter's relationship with her dad remains at the forefront of all my co-parenting decisions, day in and day out. Even when I know he's mad at me or doesn't agree with a choice I've made, ensuring that Bella maintains a positive attitude toward her dad serves to perpetuate a lasting love between father and child. I probably go heavier on this than many would, because I understand the pain of not having a father present in my life. My daughter deserves to love her dad without my bias, and your kids deserve the same.

I always have such respect for women who bite their tongues even though it burns them, knowing what it costs them to do it. Someone I worked with not long ago, whom we'll call Laura, had every reason to air her ex-husband's dirty laundry out to dry for all 750,000 of his Twitter and Instagram followers. But she zipped her lips. Laura was a hardworking professional who unfortunately found out the hard way that her husband—father to three of her young kids—had been cheating on her with a woman he met on the Internet. She insisted that she would not give in to the attempts from journalists and reporters and even

TMZ to divulge details of their split. Her ex-husband is a celebrity, and while she certainly could have gotten back at him by destroying his career or sullying his name, she put her kids first.

"I knew my kids would be so upset with me one day for putting that out in public," she told me, and I couldn't disagree with her at all.

No one, not even your closest friends and family members, deserves access to this part of your story. Marital issues are extremely personal, and you're allowed to keep these tucked away forever if you so choose.

As my name was finally called that morning in the coffee shop, I grabbed my latte, smirked, and answered my mother's friend succinctly.

"You don't have to be sorry about my divorce," I said. "I'm certainly not."

LONG STORY SHORT

+ Don't hate the Fleers; learn how to deal with the Flockers.

+ Not all your beans need to be spilled.

+ Other people's projections are not your problem. You're allowed to stand strong in your choices, even if they offend others.

JOURNAL PROMPT

Have a plan! In what ways can you comfortably answer the inevitable divorce questions that may come your way? Write a script you can follow.

CHAPTER 3

Uncomfortable Comfort: Dismantling a Family and Life as You Knew It

W hen you're facing the end of a marriage, you're thinking of you. How *you* will handle the idea of being alone. How *you* will find the strength to start over. How *you* will learn to manage co-parenting with someone who has hurt you. And who can blame you? These are things that must be thought through. You're so bogged down with these important and heavy concepts that you hardly have a moment to think of the collateral damage your divorce will cause.

This reality hit me two days after my ex moved out. I was rearranging the house, claiming the space he left when he took all his things. "Alexa, give me good vibes!" I shouted. "Playing good vibes playlist," she responded, and I had music blasting throughout the house to keep my energy up and my spirits high.

Then, by accident, I opened *the* box. The one packed tight with our wedding photos, albums, and keepsakes. Time suddenly stood still. I could feel my ears getting hot. I was transported back to that January night in Miami Beach, just three years prior, where 250 of our closest friends and family gathered to watch us become husband and wife. I winced at the memory of the nerves and anxiety I felt leading up to that moment, the signs I ignored for months.

Frame by frame, album by album, I had to keep reminding myself that a beautiful wedding does not make a beautiful marriage. *Damn, we looked good*, I thought when I saw the photo of me sitting on his lap in front of the altar. *God dammit, why couldn't you make this work, Michelle?* My gut reaction was to ask Alexa to hold the Beyoncé and play our wedding song instead, but then I came across a particular frame with multiple photos in it that stopped me in my tracks. I ordered Alexa to shut the music off entirely as my brain filled with noise. I needed a moment. In that frame was one of those classic altar photos with us, the newly married bride and groom, and every single member of our respective families. There had to be thirty of us: parents, grandparents, aunts, cousins, siblings, you name it. Everyone was beaming from ear to ear, with the happy couple sandwiched somewhere in the middle. Then, surrounding the big family photo, were snapshots with friends—other couples, ones who would have to pick and choose whether or not to still be our friends since we were now uncoupling. And I realized in that moment that we were not just cutting ties as two humans who were no longer fit to be married. We were dismantling an entire life.

I liken this dismantling to the aftershocks of an earthquake; the initial quake blasts through a city, devastating it in seconds, but the aftershocks can be felt for hundreds, if not thousands, of miles in the days thereafter, causing a ripple effect.

That's what dismantling a life after divorce is like.

As someone who's so fiercely committed to the concept of

family, someone whose values are rooted deep in family tradi-
tion and who's so committed to teaching her daughter just how
priceless family ties can be, the notion of splitting a family apart
hit hard.

I was devastated about the impact on our families, and so
damn anxious about what my split would mean for my friendships. Would I be ostracized? Supported? Feared? Banished to
divorce island, where my truth couldn't make anyone else feel
things they didn't know how to feel?

Shortly after my ex moved out, I came across an article in
the *Washington Post* that felt like it was written just for me. The
author, Samantha Shanley, talked about the loneliness and grief
that came with divorce, despite wanting and initiating the divorce. She said:

> Divorce brings about the loneliest kind of grief, with
> the death of a marriage hovering somewhere between a
> thing lost and one broken but not entirely gone. Many
> of our friends and family scattered, fearful, perhaps, of
> our emotional bardo, which had been triggered by fac-
> tors they could not possibly understand.[1]

These things, these icky feelings we try our hardest to avoid,
are inevitable in this type of situation. Divorce is icky. Splitting
apart a family is icky. Losing friendships is icky. Being the lone
single friend in a group of young couples is icky.

I was the first of my friends headed for divorce (though not
the last, of course.) The first one trudging into school events and
birthday parties without a spouse. The first who couldn't add
anything to the conversation when everyone was bitching about
their husbands at our post-carpool coffee date. The first one of

us who would be home, twiddling her thumbs on a Saturday night, debating between popping an Ambien or another couple of Dove dark chocolates into her mouth.

For the months leading up to my split, my friends would sit and listen to me cry, complain, and vent with open arms. "You've totally got this!" they'd say to reassure me. "You're so much better than him!" I'd hear. One friend's husband even promised me that they'd have my back "no matter what," when I expressed to them my fear of having to sit at home alone every Saturday night. But Saturday nights came and went, and I was very often alone, avoiding the inevitable date-night selfies on social media as best I could.

GET COMFORTABLE WITH
BEING UNCOMFORTABLE

I'm not sharing this to scare you or upset you but rather to prepare you. If you know me, you know I aim to keep it real, and there's nothing more real than sitting alone with yourself, completely still in the silence of your new reality, when it seems the rest of the world is spinning along without you. There's nothing more real than seeing which of the friends you thought you could trust the most stop reaching out to make plans, take days to respond to texts, and start posting photos with their new besties that seem to have appeared out of nowhere. There's nothing more real than your child asking why her other grandparents, your ex's parents who now curse the day you were born, can't come to holiday dinner too.

But this is the life of those moving on. These are the sacrifices we are forced to make when we decide to take our happiness into our own hands and blaze a path we never imagined blazing. This is the unfortunate price we pay for wanting more and better. I call this whole period of post-separation fuckery "the time of uncomfortable comfort," because, even though it may mean the end of life as you knew it, there's something really comforting about finally letting go of what wasn't working.

You have to get comfortable being uncomfortable. Stay with me here . . .

Years ago, at the very beginning of my entrepreneurial journey, a friend gave me a card that said, "Get comfortable being uncomfortable." We were always passing business advice back and forth, and this one took me aback at first. It sounded negative. I didn't understand the context until years later, when I found the card buried at the bottom of a desk drawer. Turns out, it originated with the US Navy SEALs. Their philosophy is that if you can get comfortable being uncomfortable, you'll be well-equipped to tackle any situation. I find it the perfect piece of wisdom for those in the early stages of divorce. Learning to live with the discomfort of a divorce means you're feeling the things you need to feel. For me, these feelings were motivating, and pushed me harder toward the good—the things I knew I wanted and had to strive for.

Get comfortable being uncomfortable with your new label. Allow yourself to feel icky for a bit if it means eventually getting you to the other side of the rainbow. Let the comfort of a marital status wash away to something far less "safe" so that you can get to where you really want to be—happy, fulfilled, *comfortable*.

ACCEPT THE SHEDDING

Have you ever watched a spaceship launch from the Kennedy Space Center? It blasts off, full of power and energy, and heads straight into outer space. Somewhere near the edge of the atmosphere, the rocket starts shedding its parts, losing what it no longer needs to reach its destination. It flies lighter, calmer, with less firepower, almost floating.

This is you. Your life is the rocket. You are the astronaut. Your happiness is the next undiscovered planet. You need to shed what no longer serves you in order to make it to this new world.

It all starts with acceptance.

Accept that familial relationships, friendships, social dynamics, and life as you knew it have just entered a new season: the shedding season. Accept that parts of your old life can no longer be attached to the rocket. Those parts served their purpose at one point or another, but now it's just smooth sailing until you get to Mars.

I decided to embrace the discomfort of the shedding. The discomfort of where I was in that moment: friendships, family ties, and bonds scattered about like the remnants of a nuclear blast. Since lonely weekend nights were my trigger, I made a choice to use Saturday nights at home alone as time that I accepted as uncomfortable, but necessary in order to heal. I found comfort in that. Instead of sitting around wallowing in pity, scrolling Instagram and unfollowing all of my friends who were sharing their "so in love with my best friend" photos from that new restaurant I had been dying to try, I made that time *my* time—to do whatever the hell made me feel better.

I read books, lots of them. I read the self-help kind, to fuel my growth, and then read the raunchy 50-shades kind, to distract me and remind myself that at least I wasn't committed to some kind of sexual deviant who got off on causing me physical pain. Weird.

I wrote. I journaled my big single-mom butt off. I made promises to myself in my writing. I tore myself apart in my writing, making peace with my flaws and vowing to do better for myself and for Bella. I watched everything and anything on Netflix, and actually enjoyed it. It was the first time in years that I was able to choose something I actually wanted to see and watch it straight through without getting lost in my thoughts or crying over the fight my ex and I had just had.

I got really comfortable in this uncomfortable time. And if I could do that, you can too.

LONG STORY SHORT

✦ Dismantling a marriage means more than just a split between two people. Collateral damage extends to friends and family.

✦ Divorce gives you the opportunity to enter a season of shedding.

✦ You will eventually learn to navigate being the lone single mama in a world of married friends.

✦ Embracing the uncomfortable comfort is a beautiful opportunity.

JOURNAL PROMPT

What are some things you can do on a lonely Saturday night after your kids are asleep that bring you good vibes?

CHAPTER 4

Getting Laid After Divorce, Part 1

I had a friend at the time of my separation who was widowed—kinda. Her husband passed away suddenly just after their split, which left her to raise their then-toddler daughter on her own. I respected her for all she had been through, and found myself especially close to her during the bleak, lonely months just before I ended my marriage. I looked to her like a beacon of hope—my own personal lighthouse in the storm I had been living in. She had lost so much, yet even through it, I could see she was enjoying life in her own way.

I also enjoyed living vicariously through her as she tore through much younger, very sexy men—mostly hot-bodied fitness trainers—and told me every last detail. She was the kind of girl that guys in this aesthetic-obsessed town couldn't turn down, with her teeny-tiny tight bod, huge fake boobs, and a lust for love. It was honestly impressive. It was so far from where I then found myself. Each time I'd see a text from her lighting up my phone, I knew I was about to be transported into another world of sex, adventure, and fun.

"Just leave him, so you can go screw whoever you want,"

she'd tell me. "You need to get under someone else so that you can get over him and get on with your life."

Screw whoever I want. Hmm. It was a fun idea, in theory, but I had serious doubts about my friend's idea of "moving on." *Am I even still fuckable?* I'd wonder, staring at myself in the mirror. I'd run my hands over my new C-section-induced belly pooch, paralyzed with fear at the idea of letting someone see my post-baby body naked, even in the dark.

Is that what I even want *to be?* I'd ask myself.

I mean, if I'm being honest, it was that kind of frivolous fun that had gotten me here in the first place. My ex-husband was good-looking, charming, a fun time at the bar, and that was all it took for me to be hooked. As someone who was never much of a prude (sorry, Mom), I would have taken my friend's advice absolutely seriously if I were still the Michelle who first entered that marriage, the girl who ignored her daddy issues (among others) and went through life attaching herself to all the wrong men.

But there was no way I could be that girl again—I knew this as soon as I had Bella. The idea of that girl made me shudder.

After all, *I was leaving this marriage because it lacked the deep personal connection, respect, and emotional security I was so desperate for.* I had already become fixated on the notion that I would much rather be alone than settle for anything less than what I knew I wanted. What I finally knew I deserved.

Then one day, I met a guy at the chiropractor's office . . .

MOMMY, PRETTY

It was a cool Saturday morning in March, all of one week since I had become single. I got Bella dressed and headed for my chiropractor's office for my early morning appointment, only to be met with a wait. I found a row of empty chairs in the waiting area and made myself comfortable, hoping to not have to make conversation or small talk with anyone. I was watching Bella bounce around from toy to toy in the play area, wondering if anyone I knew would pop in and put me on the spot. Then, the door chime rang, as if to signify that the wind was about to drag in something worth noticing.

And boy, was he ever. This tall, handsome drink of water strolled into the office, locked eyes with me, ignored all the other available chairs, and sat down right next to me.

He's either a serial killer or he's into me, I thought, secretly hoping it was the former, since I had zero flirting skills at this point in my life.

Thankfully, Bella did the flirting for me. She ran over to both of us, handed him a cookie she had somehow snagged, and crawled into my arms to play with my hair.

"How old is she?" he asked.

"She's just two," I said, and asked if he had any kids.

"Nope, not yet," he said quickly. My eyes shot down to his left hand. No ring.

"Mommy, pretty," Bella said.

"She's a very smart girl," he said, looking deep into my eyes and holding a stare that I felt in my gut.

Then, finally, the receptionist called my name.

After getting fully adjusted, I stumbled to the front desk to check out. Thinking my dream dude might be still there, I fixed my hair and hoped my mascara wasn't smudged under my eyes like it usually is after cramming my face into the hole on the table.

But he was gone. *Damn*, I thought, reliving that brief intense connection. He was hot—so hot!—in his Saturday morning sweats and white tee. And don't get me started on that cologne—oof. I was instantly rethinking all of my no-more-casual-sex rules, but like a thief in the night, he'd disappeared. What a buzzkill.

Two days later, as I was sitting in the carpool lane waiting to pick up Bella from preschool and doing my hundredth Instagram scroll of the day, I decided to check my message requests.

And there he was: *Hi, I'm the guy from the chiropractor's office. I asked for your name before I left, I hope you don't think that's creepy.*

JACKPOT! I thought.

From that moment on, we communicated endlessly. Instagram DMs turned into texts. Texts turned into late-night phone calls. Late-night phone calls turned into NSFW picture messages. We had a good flow going, but I couldn't help but wonder why he would always go out to his car to call me. "Bad service in my house," he'd say, as I pretended that wasn't super shady. Ignoring my gut like the same girl I was five years prior, it wasn't long before we made plans to hang out. I kept thinking about my wants, my needs, and what I knew I deserved. I convinced myself that somehow the stars had aligned—even if he "didn't have good service in his house"—and that I was making the next step in my life happen. I was riding a wave of pure adrenaline and fueled by my now well-stroked ego as I prepared to throw myself at this guy on our first date.

DON'T FORGET TO GOOGLE

"Tell me about him!" a friend said at lunch, as we sat with laptops open, getting some work in before picking up our girls from preschool. I hadn't yet met him for a first date, but the promise of one was looming.

I gushed. I ranted and raved. I mentioned the sweatpants and cologne, as she would know that was absolutely what did me in.

"Have you Googled him? What did you find?" she asked.

But I hadn't. I hadn't even thought about it, to be honest. It had been years since I dated.

"Oh my god, Michelle, what's wrong with you? What if he's a serial killer!" she asked.

"I already thought of that," I said, and laughed.

She asked for his first and last name and the company he worked at and started to type.

Three seconds later, we discovered that he wasn't a serial killer. He was something far worse. My dream man was—you guessed it—MARRIED, for just over one year, his wedding registry told us.

And that wasn't all, we realized, as we scrolled down to another registry. His first baby had been born the same week I met him at the chiropractor's office. *Womp, womp.*

Could I have seen the signs? Maybe. Maybe if I was thinking more clearly, had put more time between my split and the desire to be with someone new, and had taken the time to reconnect with my gut. Maybe.

I'm not telling you that you can't scratch that itch. Please, by all means, do what you gotta do to feel good. But know yourself. Understand that your emotions are raw and that you're currently more vulnerable than usual. It may make you miss the red flags waving right in front of your face—like the guy who seems to never call you from his house. Accept that letting it all go, even for just one night, could leave you feeling even worse than before.

Ask yourself these questions before you ask that booty call to come over later on tonight:

1. Will I feel better or worse about myself if I sleep with this person and never hear from him again?

2. Am I really looking to get laid, or am I looking for validation that someone still finds me attractive?

3. Is it really revenge sex if your ex isn't ever going to find out about it?

And perhaps the biggest question of all,

4. If I use sex to make myself feel better, will be I falling back into old, unhealthy patterns?

Years later, I came across an article in O, The Oprah Magazine about sex after divorce, when I was helping a client through her own issues. She was trying to figure out whether or not to reconnect with an old flame who was paying her lots of attention after hearing about her divorce. Naturally, she wanted to dive headfirst into this opportunity, and who could blame her? This kind of attention feels pretty damn good after having been emotionally neglected for so long!

But I had a sneaking suspicion that she truly wasn't ready for this, after all she had endured. It was important to me that she not find herself taking three steps back emotionally just to satisfy her need for some human touch. This quote from Dr. Shannon Chavez, a Los Angeles-based psychologist and sex therapist, basically summed up what I already knew to be true:

The element of vulnerability after a divorce is undeniable. If there has been a lot of conflict or rejection throughout the marriage, a person may have taken major hits to their self-esteem. So, even if you're eager to find a new partner, it's often wise to take a deep breath and start to rebuild the way you see yourself before looking outward.[1]

Baby steps, Mama. The sex will feel so much better once you're healed and ready for it.

SWIPE RIGHT?

Per your well-meaning friends' advice, you may find yourself downloading an app like Tinder or Hinge or whatever the most popular new swipe-to-meet-your-destiny app is at the moment. I know it seems tempting, at least just this once. Your curiosity might lead you astray, digging deep into the depths of the online dating mystery world just to see who you'd attract or who would end up in your in-box with a "hey baby" message and a promise of a good time. I can promise you that the self-confidence boost of knowing someone swiped right on your profile will fade to self-doubt if you go through with the hookup too soon. "Why didn't he call?" "Was it me?" "Oh god, it definitely had to be me."

You'll obsess over someone you probably never would have thought about otherwise, and you'll doubt yourself before you've even given yourself a chance to step into your power. You'll shoot yourself in the foot before the big race. This kind of disappointment and distraction is not what you need right now.

Slow and steady, Mama—you'll get there, and it'll feel that much better when you're ready for it.

LONG STORY SHORT

✦ You're going to want to have sex, all of it, since you likely haven't felt much passion in a while.

✦ You won't be ready to do this until you've healed.

✦ Hopefully, when you do it, it won't be with someone who's hiding the fact that he has a new wife and baby boy at home.

✦ The best sex is the kind you feel confident, comfortable, and emotionally ready for.

JOURNAL PROMPT

When was the last time you felt truly emotionally safe in an intimate situation? Do you feel ready for that again? Why or why not?

CHAPTER 5

Misery Loves Company: But Friends Are for More than That

"T ell me everything," was how each conversation with a friend I will call Jane would start. I would—whine, complain, throw fire. "Ugh, he's the worst," she'd add to the end of each of my sentences. I felt validated. Seen. Heard. And before long, I found myself going to Jane with every painful and brutal detail of how my marriage was unraveling. She called multiple times a day to "check in." She wanted to be the first call after each lawyer's visit. She let me cry to her, vent to her, and just about anything else I needed to do.

"How does she have this much time to deal with your problems?" my mom once asked, stinging me to my core.

Ew, Ma. Rude.

I felt lucky to have Jane as a friend, even if she *was* in another state. We'd chat all day and FaceTime when I was especially on the edge. It felt good to be this connected to someone during such a lonely period of my life. I mean, I did wonder how her husband felt about all this time she spent unpacking my bullshit, but, nonetheless, I still felt lucky that there was someone who had my back as fiercely as she did—who was happy to take in every moment with me as it came.

Only it turned out she wasn't happy to take in *every* moment with me as it came. *But I didn't see that yet.*

My friend was the quintessential got-your-back friend. I had known her since before I could walk, and she always seemed to pop back into my life when shit was headed south for me. In fact, whenever anyone she knew was going through something difficult, she was right there for them, too. She was knee deep in the swamp with me now, but I never stopped to realize that she enjoyed other people's swamps because of what was going on in her own life. She wasn't the type to vent her problems to others, but here and there, in between my incessant whining and crying, I'd get glimpses into her own unhappiness.

"Can you talk?" I'd ask when calling late at night.

"Of course I can; it's not like my husband came home yet or anything like that," she'd respond sarcastically.

"Are you busy with the kids?" I'd ask when calling on a weekend.

"When am I not? I feel like a single mother too," she'd quip back.

She was dropping bread crumbs like Hansel and Gretel on their way into the forest. I was just too sucked into my own quicksand to realize it.

Naturally, she was my first phone call after my first date with my now-husband. I remember being so excited for morning to come so I could finally spill my guts to her. I had barely woken up before my phone was in hand. As I shared every last detail, with joy in my voice for the first time in years, her tone got more and more dismissive. She cut me off mid-sentence, claiming she had someone at her door. And this was only the beginning of the end.

EMOTIONAL CONTAGION

It was a slow decline that I had probably been ignoring for a while. We'd still have our check-ins, only now, the questions about my "hot Miami love affair" were distinctly passive-aggressive, and each response more sarcastic than the last. I'd mention how I thought he was the one, only for her to imply I was living in la-la land and moving too quickly. "Is that what people do down there in Florida?" she'd ask. I couldn't, for the life of me, understand what the hell was going on.

"I told you something wasn't right," my mom said to me, proud to prove me wrong. "Misery loves company, Michelle, and she has no use for you anymore now that you're happy."

My mom reminded me of her own "best friend," who stood by her side after my stepdad passed away. My mom was in a really broken place after his passing, and this friend seemed to always be there: for lunch, for a stroll in the mall, to listen to her cry. Until my mom met her third husband. Then this friend stopped answering her phone.

Holy shit, I thought. How did I not see this? This friend was just like my mother's had been. She'd lapped up every last drop of my misery like a starving puppy, and here I was, just letting her feed off my drama and misery. She got high on it. She literally came looking for it every day. Like some sort of emotional exorcist, she'd let me expel my demons to her.

Perhaps this woman wasn't my friend. She was an emotional contagion, clinging to my virus of unhappiness to fuel her own unhappy life.

It wasn't long before she cut me off completely—just months after I shared with her that my romance with Spencer had started heating up and we'd begun the process of looking for a home. It hurt. It stung. But I should have seen it coming.

"Told ya," my mom said again.

It wasn't like this woman was my only friend at that time. I had (and have) plenty of friends—happy ones who didn't hover, but were always there when I needed them. I realize now that, as adult women in our thirties, with children, and jobs, and a whole boatload of other fish to fry, it wasn't anyone's job to hover. A good friend made it known that she was there if needed but carried on with her own life. Unlike this friend, who invested 400 percent of her time into my life as a means to escape from her own reality—a reality she was too sad to face. I soon learned her husband had lost his job again, was caught texting with an ex, and inevitably ended up leaving her. And that's precisely what you need to be on the lookout for: the healthy balance friends, not the Flocker who needs to live through your own misery to distract from her own unhappy life, and who abandons you just when you're on the road to being your best, happiest self.

SELL MISERY SOMEPLACE ELSE, WE'RE ALL STOCKED UP HERE

When it comes to your energy, time, and ability to trust again after enduring a traumatic life experience such as divorce, think of yourself as a flower in a dark room. You're understandably vulnerable right now, and in need of someone to lean on and help turn on the light. There's only so much of you to go around as you're burning the candle at both ends, trying to navigate single motherhood, the divorce process, work, and whatever else is on your plate. You have only so much ability to tolerate darkness: the friends who refuse to help you turn the light on but would rather sit with you while you wither away. You have to recognize which friends are willing to flip that switch for you, and which enjoy the dark. You must accept that when it comes to friendships, this isn't college spring break. *More* friends isn't the goal. It's quality that matters now.

Having had more than my fair share of toxic friendships throughout the years, I can attest that it took just as much self-awareness and inner work to spot energy-vampire friends as it did to recognize men who were bad for me. Emotional bonds are emotional bonds are emotional bonds. Just because some relationships don't involve sex doesn't mean they aren't intimate, and that your triggers and patterns don't come into play. So protecting yourself should be a priority.

LET 'EM GO

Here's a look at different kinds of friends and how to avoid (or gently separate from) the ones that will hurt you. The goal is to make sure your friendships are truly serving you—a wise goal anytime, but especially when you're going through such a profound change.

The Emotional Contagion Friend

This is your Jane—way too invested, making you feel like a fish in a fishbowl, with nowhere to hide. Friends like this question what you're doing all the time, why you did it, what you're wearing, and are the first to criticize or chastise you when they get an answer that challenges their current state of existence. It's perfectly okay to have supportive friends, but it's never okay for any friends to feel they can control your every move. If you meet someone who reminds you of the overbearing mother/boyfriend/MIL that you can't get away from quickly enough, take heed!

The Overnight Bestie

Talk about red flag express. Did you ever meet someone who, right off the bat, started texting you incessantly as if you'd been best friends for years? I've had a bunch of these, but I've always chalked it up to my big mouth and ability to make conversation with anyone. These friends attach themselves quickly, usually out of insecurity, and want you all to themselves. They want to make plans every single day, and have plans set for the next day before you split the tab on dinner. As you start to pull away, or involve other friends in your life, they become jealous and clingy—and who needs that kind of energy right now?

The Evil-Eye Friend

It's been two years since I moved into my new home with my new husband, and there's a certain friend in particular whom I still haven't invited over for coffee. Why not? Each time I see her, she seems to take a full inventory of me—what I'm wearing, the size of my engagement ring, what car I'm driving—and offers up a must-be-nice kind of review. Her intense scrutiny makes me feel as though she can jinx me. This makes me nervous, as I'm admittedly crazy superstitious and believe in the evil eye—a symbol that's meant to protect you from anyone who's jealous and sending "evil" vibes your way. There's always some tone of jealousy in her voice, followed by a "but I'm sooooo happy for you" blanket statement, and it always makes me feel icky afterward. Keep this kind of friend at arm's length—you don't need anyone throwing bad energy your way.

The Debbie Downer

She's as negative as the day is long, kind of like my emotional-contagion friend. Her kids? She can't stand them. Her husband? Ugh, what a slob. Her job? She hopes and prays to be fired. It seems as if nothing makes her happy, and she wants to keep you right down there with her. Run, Forrest, RUN. You deserve joy in your life right now, Mama, and this is the kind of friend who will prevent it at every turn, because, ahem, misery loves company.

KEEP 'EM CLOSE

It's no secret that your roster of go-to people will change when your marital status does. Once you've carefully analyzed the friends that add value to your life and weeded out the ones that keep you down and hold you back, it's pretty liberating.

Here are the kind of friends to keep close during this time in your life—the ones who will inevitably be around forever:

The Good Listener

You're going to have a lot to say. You'll have lots of feelings, doubts, concerns, and it'll all need to go somewhere. Aside from your therapist, it's really important to have a friend who listens. This is the one who you know isn't keeping you on speaker as she does twelve other things, but instead wants to make you feel heard even if she hasn't the first clue about divorce or how to advise you. It's always a confidence booster to know you're cared about, and having someone who's happy to listen to you is a great way to feel the love.

The Friend with Boundaries

You know who I've found the best kind of friends to have are? The ones with boundaries. The ones who can say, "Sorry I didn't answer your call, I was getting the kids to bed and then desperately needed a glass of wine and some silence. I love you and I want to catch up tomorrow!" And who actually do call tomorrow. These are the good ones. They know their own personal limits, which means they can bring the best of themselves to the table when you need it. I've learned a lot from my friends with clear boundaries, and respect and admire them the most of all—they're my lifers, no doubt. Your divorce may be the center of *your* universe, but you can't expect your emotionally well-balanced friends to act as though it's the center of theirs. As we've seen, those who do are likely harboring their own hurts.

The Friend Who Gets It

Who better to understand what you're going through right now than someone who has been there before? This is the type of friendship that will give you hope and courage as you weather your divorce storm, because it's with someone who has made it to the end of her own divorce journey and is still emotionally intact and thriving at life. A friendship like this is motivating, full of wisdom, and—hopefully—full of good energy too. The been-there-done-that perspective will keep you hanging on through your darkest divorce days, and this is the kind of friend who will say, "I told you so," in the best way possible, with each hurdle you overcome.

If you're worried that these kinds of friends are hard to find, fear not. As you reinvent yourself during this phase of your life, the universe will bring you support in all forms, whether you expect it or not. If you approach this new chapter of your life with open eyes and arms, you'll find yourself gravitating toward exactly what is right for you right now. Women are amazing like that. In times of sadness or crisis, we vent, we go to therapy, we read self-help books, we join Facebook groups, we ask questions, we level up, and we learn our worth. Unlike (some) men, we mostly don't try to face everything alone. We reach out for help: new friends, old friends, whatever.

I repeat: Women are amazing like that.

LONG STORY SHORT

+ Not all friendships are healthy for you right now.

+ Beware of friends that are too clingy, too judgmental, or too hooked into your life and problems.

+ Find the friends that truly listen, that keep healthy boundaries, and that know what you're going through.

+ Don't underestimate your ability to bring the kind of people into your life right now that you need most.

+ Trust the universe.

JOURNAL PROMPT

Are there any friends in your life that fit the "emotional contagion" description? How do you know? What can you do to make sure they don't hurt you? Let's do a friend inventory to help make sure you're surrounded by the best people, with only the best intentions for you.

CHAPTER 6

Two Hands and Too Much to Handle—Single Parenting Survival Tips

Y ou knew it'd be hard, physically. Taking care of children, especially the younger kind with boundless energy and little ability to see to any of their basic human needs—it's pretty much an Olympic sport, in my humble opinion. Taking care of them all by your damn self, when there's suddenly no one else to lean on for support, a pee break, or a helping hand to clean up that fourth spilled juice box of the day? That's a whole other level of *what the fuck did I just get myself into?* It takes things from being a difficult physical feat to an emotionally draining one as well. Not only is there no one to download with, you're pissed— resentful of the situation you've been put in, and consumed with the question of "why."

Why me?

Why now?

Why us?

Why? Why? WHY!??!?

STOP WHY'ING ALL OVER YOURSELF

You're in it now, and you're doing it day by day, whether you like it or not. The "why" of your situation—whether you chose to be on your own or whether you were left by the person you loved—is of no consequence now. I hate to break it to you, but it's true. Because you have no choice. You don't have a time machine, magic wand, or mind-eraser cream that can reverse whatever led you to this point.

But you *do* have children, and I don't need to remind you that you are their world. It's a lot of pressure, I get it. I've been there, and while I wasn't in that position for long, it was still hard as hell. I found my way, what worked for me, and how to quiet the criticism from those around me about how I was parenting (read: surviving) on my own.

Settling into life as a single parent means untying yourself from the why—as painful as your "why" may be—if you want to have any shot at moving forward with strength instead of resentment. Resentment doesn't help an already difficult situation, believe you me. Repeat this to yourself, right now, out loud. Don't worry—no one's looking:

> My relationship with my ex may be over, but my relationship with my children is not. It's about to become stronger than ever, because they need and deserve that.

Now, I bet you're expecting a recipe for self-care here, a dash of you-time sprinkled in with multiple daily positive affirmation sessions, layered with mindful meditation. Don't get me wrong, all of those things are wonderful, but if we're talking single parenting, it's going to take letting yourself go a bit deeper into your own personal needs and zooming in real tight to the here and now, instead of swallowing this giant chunk of responsibility with one bite. You'll need a hell of a lot more creativity, and some good old-fashioned strategy, to make your new solo parenting game a good one.

MOMMY, YOU NAKED

I hear moms complain all the time about wanting to take a shower in peace. This takes on a whole new meaning when you're alone with a toddler and desperate for a good rinse. Sure, there were plenty of days when I would wait until Bella was asleep to spend an excessive amount of time under the pressure of the hot water, letting it wash away the stress of my day. But then there were times when, after having been at the playground in the midday Miami heat for hours on end, I just needed a quick rinse to reset my mood and prepare me for the rest of the day. There's one day in particular that I'll never, ever forget. This is the day that perfectly epitomizes the delicate balancing act of being a single mom with a toddler.

I don't recall what day of the week it was, but I remember Bella and I had been invited to attend a family dinner that night. We had been to the park after a morning of running errands, and it would have been downright disrespectful of me to show up to my aunt's home unshowered and with park germs seeping from my pores. My first attempt at having a moment to myself that day had failed. I drove around my neighborhood for just about an hour to get Bella to sleep so that I could lay her in her crib while I got myself ready. She fell asleep peacefully in the backseat of my Jeep, only to be woken up by my neighbor's yappy Chihuahua as I gently carried her out of the car and into my house.

Well, shit, I thought. *There goes that.*

Not one to give up without a fight, I decided to get creative. I brought a whole heap of toys into my bathroom and plopped them on the floor. I threw good ol' *Peppa Pig* up on the iPad and propped up the screen so she could watch it as she played. All of a sudden, she was just about distracted enough for me to rip off my sweaty sports bra and leggings and get at least a minute under the warm, wet reprieve. I felt like a champ. I had successfully found a way to shower with Bella awake for the first time as a single mom. I looked over at her banging her Doc McStuffins microphone onto the bathroom floor to the beat of the *Peppa Pig* theme song, and decided I even had time to shave my legs. A little too ambitious, maybe. I would soon be eating my words. Somewhere between plucking the shaving cream can off my shower ledge and lathering on the goods, I managed to drop it, right out of my wet, soapy hands, straight down onto the shower floor, scaring the bejesus out of Bella and distracting her from her bathroom-floor babysitters.

And just like that, she was on the run.

Oh my good god, I thought. Had I latched the gate at the top of the stairs? Was she about to plummet headfirst into an almost-certain emergency room situation? My mind raced with what-ifs, and visions of X-ray machines danced through my head as I jumped out of the shower—only to realize I hadn't brought in a clean towel from the laundry room.

Bare-naked, dripping wet, and with shaving cream slathered up to my knee on one lonely leg, I tore through my house like a bat out of hell in search of Bella. The gate was open, which meant only one thing: there was no way she was staying upstairs, and I would most certainly have to go streaking down, hoping and praying the curtains were drawn in the living room. (They weren't, but that was another issue.)

"BELLAAAAA!" I yelled, way more dramatically than I likely needed to.

Then I heard a giggle coming from my pantry.

"Boo," she said in her sweet little voice as she popped open the pantry door. "Mommy, you naked!"

I picked her up and held her tight, crying as she laughed. I just wanted a fucking shower.

Showering wasn't the only challenge I faced, of course. There was getting us both out the door in the morning on time so that she could get to preschool and I could get to work. There was the panic of forgetting to send something important in her backpack to school, imagining the teachers would roll their eyes and chalk it up to me being a distracted, sorry, single mom. There was the constant fear of not having enough money to pay my rent on my own. There was just wanting five fucking minutes of quiet time to answer an email or listen to a voice mail or just stare into space while I caught my breath. Parenting a two-year-old by myself felt like a constant game of pin-the-tail-on-the-donkey, only the donkey kept moving, and I had no arms.

Instead of trying to be supermom, I became survival-mode mom. It may sound only logical from the outside, but it was an especially difficult shift for a Type A control freak like me. I was always desperate to do motherhood perfectly, probably even more so after the split. I had nothing to prove to anyone, but still felt like I should, and it was eating me alive. I had to accept that that ship had sailed, and so would my sanity if I didn't take it easier on myself. Eventually, I leaned into how hard this whole endeavor really was and tried to do my best with every challenge that arose, even if it meant letting the iPad babysit while I took a break.

Now, while I can't wave a magic wand and make single parenting the easiest thing you've ever done, I can give you some tips and tricks to take the edge off. Consider this your single-mama blueprint for how to not lose your mind.

ROUTINES WILL SAVE YOU

Single mama, meet routine, your new best friend. You two are about to go everywhere together, spend hours on the phone catching up, and won't be able to function without each other. Creating a structure and routine not only lets your children know what to expect (which can be especially comforting to them right now), it takes any element of surprise out of your day, which benefits you just as much. If you have a toddler who makes getting out the door in the morning a whole circus act, lay out outfits, make lunches, and have backpacks packed and ready to go the night before.

Financial routines are possible too. You're likely toting your kids around while you do all your errands now, and if you have children that love a treat from the drive-through or a toy from Target when you're out and about, take the added financial pressure off your shoulders and pick a day each month where this fits into the routine. Since I rarely had the opportunity to do errands without Bella, and she always wanted every shiny item on the shelf in Target, I'd let her point to a day on the calendar and make that "Bella's shopping day" so there were no surprise meltdowns for her (or me) in the store on the days that were not earmarked for a treat.

ASK FOR ALL THE HELP

Again, no one is expecting you to be supermom right now, except maybe you! Let go of the idea that you're bothering anyone by requesting a lifeline. Adjusting to life as a single parent in a healthy way means knowing when to ask for help, and who to lean on for support. If you have family nearby, take advantage! That cousin who keeps asking to watch your little one whenever you need a hand—reach out. Your mom, who always calls and asks if you need anything from her trip to Costco—don't be shy, ask for it. The neighbor who's always cooking and offers to drop off some goodies she's made—say yes. The friend who has offered to come sit with your children so that you can, in fact, shower in peace—hold her close and never let her go.

If these aren't viable options for you, know when to outsource the help. Because I function best with peace of mind and routine, I hired an amazing sitter for Bella right after my separation. I didn't always have somewhere to be on Wednesday evenings at 6 p.m., but I knew that every Wednesday at 6 p.m., come hell or high water, she'd be at my house with a heart full of love and a bag full of treats for Bella, so that I could finally run to Home Goods and return that useless purchase or take a walk around my neighborhood to clear my head. That felt good—really good—and was worth every penny spent. I know not everyone has a lot of extra money for sitters, but for me, that occasional peace of mind was so much more valuable than any other luxury I might have been considering—I would forgo a year's worth of shopping in a second. Think about whether there are any other treats you can redirect toward a sitter, even just for a few hours a week—I promise you'll thank yourself!

SET A BUDGET AND STICK TO IT

I'll be honest: for a long time, I was the worst with money, budgeting, and avoiding frivolous spending. I made money, I spent it, and I lived as though my next paycheck was guaranteed. For a while, I got away with it, because there was someone else alongside me earning too.

And then there wasn't. I started building my marketing business well in advance of my split, knowing full well that I'd need a way to take care of myself and Bella when the shit hit the fan. I was determined to make money so that I'd have nothing to worry about, but I soon learned that, when it comes to managing your own business, there's *always* something to worry about.

Fast-forward a year or so and I was on my own, with a rent payment that was a bit of a reach, my daughter's private preschool to pay for, and all the other expenses that come with raising a kid. Each time I thought about money—earning enough, losing a client, missing a payment—my chest would tighten, and I'd fall into a panic. I'd fling open my laptop to check my bank accounts and write a list of each thing that still needed to be paid for that month.

Yeah, so this is why budgeting is a big deal.

Talk about adulting. I made a list of all the money I'd need to spend on a monthly basis. I started with my "must pay" list: my rent, car, phone and insurance payments, along with school tuition and the legal fees I was now incurring. I followed that up with the fun stuff: lunch with clients, dinner with friends. And then I had to do the uncomfortable thing: tally up my Starbucks visits and follow that up with a facepalm. With this realization, the frivolous spending took a backseat to feeling empowered and in control of my budget.

DO NOT IGNORE YOUR MENTAL HEALTH

I know you feel the weight of the world on your shoulders right now. How could you not? This single-parent pressure often comes entangled in a desperate desire to be supermom, to do things perfectly and leave no room for error. You feel like you have something to prove: to your ex, to the family that swore you couldn't do this on your own, and most of all, *to yourself.* Well, if you're driving 100 miles per hour day after day, without so much as a pit stop for gas and a snack, you're eventually going to burn out and find yourself stuck on the side of the road, begging for help.

I recently had the pleasure of meeting Sheva Ganz, a single-mom coach with three kids who left a marriage and a strict religious culture in search of true happiness—and I was inspired in ways I hadn't been for some time. I asked her questions about how she did it, how she mustered up the courage and managed to take care of three children at the same time. Here's what she had to say:

As a single mother of three, a failure at marriage *and* Orthodox Judaism, I knew it was time to reassess my life plans (or, more aptly, the plans that had been laid out for me) and take a more godly approach to life's unpredictability. My upbringing, which stressed the importance of marriage, motherhood, and family life, had left me ill-equipped for the harsh realities of single parenting and financial responsibilities. But if God could laugh at my life gone awry, why couldn't I?

She helped me shift my perspective on failure and think about how I could instead embrace it with curiosity, self-compassion, and humor. Look around you: do you know anyone who's perfect or who leads a perfect life? I certainly don't, and I believe that our fear of failure is one of the biggest reasons we feel so much stress and anxiety. It's only natural that life is going to feel completely overwhelming if we believe we have to do everything perfectly, all the time. Failure is how we learn, grow, and develop self-awareness. However, accepting failure doesn't mean giving up, abandoning ambition, or disregarding ideals. One of my new favorite mantras is "I'm doing my best *and* I can do better," which gave me permission to accept my imperfections while challenging myself to learn from my mistakes. Slowly, as I healed and became emotionally stronger, I started to look at life like a game of Super Mario Brothers: if I "fell to my death," how could I come back stronger and more strategic, while also still enjoying the fun? I looked at challenges as opportunities, even if nothing more than a reminder that I can do hard things, that all things pass, and that if God was having a good time up there, so could I.

YOUR TURN

Slow down. Turn on cruise control. There's no rush, no prize for world's best single mom. You don't win by doing too much. You win by honoring yourself and your needs.

In my work with clients, I've often found that this desire to do it all and ask for nothing in return is really a means to distract from something, that *something* usually being the pain of their current reality. It's as if filling up a to-do list and going to bed with each task done can take your mind off the divorce. It can't. Distractions only push the pain, the reality, the guilt, deeper and deeper into your soul, making it impossible to remove and work through. There's no amount of responsibility you can take on right now that will quiet the emotional stuff you have to work through. Only therapy and honoring your emotions can do that. Remember to pause—frequently—and ask yourself how you're feeling.

Exhausted? Save the laundry for tomorrow and curl up in bed with your remote.

Resentful and angry? Say no to the next task that comes your way and grab your journal instead—start venting.

Can't stop feeling sad? TALK TO SOMEONE—ANYONE.

Going to scream if these kids ask you for one more snack? *Call in a lifeline, ship those kiddos out the door, and take a damn nap.*

LONG STORY SHORT

✦ Parenting alone isn't easy, but you've got this.

✦ Stop focusing on your why and put your energy into what is.

✦ Do things that make you feel in control: sticking to a routine, sticking to a budget, and asking for help.

✦ Being survival-mode mom is enough; stop trying to be supermom.

✦ Make your mental health a priority.

JOURNAL PROMPT

List three ways you can simplify your routine and take some stress out of your day-to-day life.

CHAPTER 7

Surviving the First Weekend Without Your Kids

The noise that has become your life since your split is deafening. It's a full-blown Level 10, bass and all. The worries racing through your brain drown out everything else. You've been running on fumes, trying to handle life as a single mom with kids to care for on your own, seven days a week, twenty-four hours a day.

You're desperate for a good night's sleep, a moment to yourself, and some goddamn peace and quiet. A night without kids sounds ideal—until it hits you: they're leaving you. For *him*. They're off to spend their very first night away from you since your split, in the care of a man you may no longer trust or like very much. Panic sets in as you start to wonder: What will it feel like? How will I get through it? Before you know it, they're gone, and you get that moment to yourself, some peace and quiet. And it doesn't feel good at all.

There's no gut punch quite like that first night alone, without your kids.

Suddenly, you miss the chaos. Your soul aches for it. You wander your house aimlessly, searching for a sense of purpose without having little tushies to wipe or crusts to cut off with laser-like precision. Each glimpse into your kids' empty rooms sends you to the floor, clutching your heart and wondering, "HOW WILL I EVER GET USED TO THIS?"

Well, Mama, spoiler alert: you'll get used to this. Not because you want to, but because you have to, whether you like it or not. But it will take time.

This is one of the most frequent questions I get in my DMs. "Please tell me it gets easier. I don't know if I can do this. How can I survive my life without my kids?"

There's a reason. It's because we're mothers, nurturers by nature, and fierce protectors of our offspring. It's in the fabric of our DNA to fight tirelessly for our children, giving them everything we have, without question. It's called maternal instinct, and it's one of the most powerful forces in the world.

In a Japanese study conducted in the late 2000s and reported on by the *New York Times*, researchers using functional magnetic resonance imaging studied the brain patterns of thirteen mothers, each with a sixteen-month-old infant. They looked at the brain patterns of the mother when presented with images of her child in distress or crying out for her. As you can imagine, the brain waves went from cool, calm, and collected to magnitude 7 on the Richter scale.[1] We are biologically designed to care for our kids, so much so that our brains have an actual reaction when we don't get that opportunity.

Just like science says, when our kids are carted off to a weekend at dad's—so unnaturally ripped from our clutches—we are left feeling empty. And because we can't actually see them, we are *imagining* them sad and lonely, missing us.

What you're feeling is all so normal, Mama.

My first full weekend without Bella didn't come until

months into my separation. We had waited until her dad got set up in his new apartment before starting overnights, but regardless, I wasn't ready. Bella was still in diapers, and completely dependent on me. She lived a life of routine, structure, and consistency in my care, and the Type A mama in me crumbled at the thought of all the ways her life might be different at Dad's. I knew he'd love and care for her as deeply as I did, just differently. But that wasn't enough to comfort me—yet.

This first weekend came on hard and fast, with little warning and even less time for me to emotionally prepare.

It was the most difficult 2,880 minutes of my entire life.

I had my friends to call and cry to, the ones who had been trying to lift me up until this point with all that you've-got-this-girl bullshit. Calling them was helpful to a point, but they didn't understand what this was truly like. How could they? Adjusting to life as a co-parent after divorce is something you cannot possibly fathom unless you're living it. You count your lucky stars that you have friends on the other end of the line listening to you, but you know deep down they have no way to relate. It's not their fault.

I spent the whole weekend with a pit in my stomach and an ache in my heart. It makes me instantly anxious just remembering it.

Here's a snippet of what went through my mind, and what many divorced moms fixate on that first weekend without kids:

WHAT IF . . .

✦ He doesn't put them to bed at the same time I do?

✦ He forgets to do that thing they love right before bedtime?

+ He doesn't make them brush their teeth?

+ He lets them eat candy to their heart's content because he's trying to be the cool dad?

+ He doesn't let them call me?

+ They miss me and he doesn't do anything to make them feel better?

+ My child says something horrible about me and he agrees?

+ He introduces them to a new woman before I'm okay with it?

+ He doesn't wake up in the morning because he died in his sleep and my little babies are left to fend for themselves? (Yes, I had this thought for more weekends than I'd like to admit.)

+ I die in my sleep and don't get the chance to say goodbye to the lives I've created?

OH GOD, KILL ME.

Looking back, I wish I had all the knowledge and strategies I implement now with my clients, to talk myself off that hideously dramatic ledge. But you don't know what you don't know. Which is why I'm preparing you for this first weekend without your kids, or the next time you miss them so deeply that you feel your heart might explode.

Let's revisit those worries:

What if he doesn't put them to bed at the same time I do?

They will survive. The world will keep on turning. They still have just as much opportunity to make it in life, despite a change in bedtime.

What if he forgets to do that thing they love right before bedtime?

Then he will do his own thing with them right before bedtime, which will in turn become their new routine with Dad and something they'll associate with sleeping at his house. A bonus, in the long run.

What if he doesn't make them brush their teeth?

They will survive. The world will keep on turning. They still have just as much opportunity to make it in life despite a missed toothbrushing session. Plus, you then reserve the right to tell him off when the kids get their first cavities. Fun!

Just kidding, please don't tell him off—you've come so far!

What if he lets them eat candy to their heart's content because he's trying to be the cool dad?

They will survive. The world will keep on turning. They still have just as much opportunity to make it in life despite their sugar-rush parties with Dad.

What if he doesn't let them call me?

This is major. I felt this and lived it in my own childhood, and I know many of you have too. Before establishing any parental time-sharing opportunities, insist that daily phone calls and/ or FaceTime opportunities are written into your parenting plan (more on that later). Your kids will miss you, they'll need to still feel connected to you, and you are not to sign a damn thing on your divorce papers until this rule is established.

What if they miss me and he doesn't do anything to make them feel better?

Your kids will inevitably miss you, and this will be a tough situation for your ex and your kids alike. But everyone, including the kids, will settle into their new reality. Eventually, your ex will learn to understand that Mama Bear is always number one, and that the kids missing you is nothing to feel threatened by. Give him time to adjust too; he's (probably) never done this before either.

What if my child says something horrible about me and he agrees?

News flash: even if you had stayed married, your kids would eventually enter puberty, in which case they will hate you at one point or another. And then they'll get over it (and you will too).

What if he introduces them to a new woman before I'm okay with it?

This one stings. Big time. But, unfortunately, there's nothing you can do at this point. If she's not a direct emotional or physical threat to your kids, the best you can do is "keep the enemy close." Why? Your ex has likely told this new woman all about you, and I don't mean the good stuff. She's expecting you to freak out about her, to her, and whenever you see her, but this is exactly what *not* to do. You need to let her know that you're willing to work together for the kids. If you curse her existence, especially in front of your kids, they will be very anxious and uncomfortable spending time with her. Let's use a little forward thinking here and help you take the high road.

Having another woman around your kids may feel like a threat, but in fact (again, unless she is somehow a physical or emotional threat), it's not such a terrible thing to have someone with a female perspective, and quite possibly a mother's intuition, around your children. The sooner you can embrace this, the sooner you can make this woman your ally and build a bridge between you and your kids when they're with your ex and the new woman.

What if he doesn't wake up in the morning because he died in his sleep and my little babies are left to fend for themselves?
Okay, well, this would be tragic—I'll give you that. But it's highly unlikely to happen and more likely that your ex will die by . . . Sorry, I'll stop.

What if I die in my sleep and don't get the chance to say goodbye to the lives I've created?
This would also be tragic and is also highly unlikely, so all you can do anyway—whether you're divorced or not—is to love them the best you can every moment you're with them, and give thanks for the time you have.

Now that we've put your worries in perspective, here are my tried-and-true strategies for making it through the first weekend without your kids:

Call your go-to people.
While your friends may not fully understand your pain, they can totally help you fill the void for the weekend. Don't be afraid

to let them know that you really and truly need them now, and some friend time is crucial for your weekend survival. Even if they're busy married moms, sitting on a friend's couch with a glass of wine or a cup of tea works just as well as going to dinner and pounding shots to numb the pain. Feeling supported and less alone is the key here, and it's who you're with—not what you're doing—that matters.

Book time with yourself.

Self-care for the win. Splurge. Do the thing you never get to do, whether it's a mani/pedi, massage, or twelve-hour-long Netflix binge in bed, the best and most affordable indulgence there is. And don't do it just on that first weekend. Make it a habit. In my first few months of adjusting to co-parenting, I spent my weekends without Bella sleeping in, taking my favorite Pilates class, and then spending the rest of the day in bed binge-watching *The Affair* on Showtime. It was therapeutic beyond words. I went from dreading the weekends without her to knowing that alone time was critical for me to be able to rebound from all the drama that comes with the divorce process.

Develop your own weird routine.

I spent an ungodly amount of time at Home Goods, after having frozen yogurt with a friend, on the first night Bella was with her dad. I filled up a cart full of décor I knew my ex would have never approved of, and I bought the shit out of it. Everything was pink and gold and shiny and emblazoned with empowering quotes. It comforted me, so I kept going back. I made it my routine (exercising more restraint on the subsequent trips, of course).

Side note: Racking up credit card bills when you're facing divorce is hardly a wise choice. Your credit card statements will be presented in court, and you want to show smart decision-making, such as "any money I receive from my ex will be used for our children and not that great new pair of slides." You'll also need that money for lawyer's bills, managing your new household, and emergency Instacart deliveries (remember the Pedialyte!).

Don't fear being alone.
Alone is where you find yourself, even if it hurts. It's where you get the opportunity to rediscover yourself more deeply, far beneath the surface of "divorcee" or "mom" or "insert job title." Your first weekend alone will be a huge learning curve, but if you can lean into it, it'll give you much-needed time to catch your breath. This is where you create the space for growth and magic.

LONG STORY SHORT

+ The first weekend without your kids will be hard.

+ They won't die, and neither will you.

+ Lean in to anyone who can help you pass the time.

+ Self-care the shit out of your weekend.

+ Go to Home Goods—even if it's just to browse.

+ Don't fear being alone.

JOURNAL PROMPT

Write down your biggest when-the-kids-are-with-dad fears. Why do you feel this way? How can you shift this catastrophic way of thinking to something more positive?

CHAPTER 8

Parenting in Pieces: Surviving Your Time Without the Kids from Now On

That first weekend without the kids? It's only the start. You're in the midst of one of the most ironic series of events you'll ever experience. Let's review it in a nutshell:

1. You find a partner you want to spend your life with.

2. You get pregnant. Hear the baby's heartbeat for the first time and vow that you'll never be anything but everything for this child. Prepare to give her everything you've got.

3. You have your baby. Begin to nurture and care for something more deeply than anything that ever came before her. Find awe and pleasure in the fact that being a mother comes so naturally to you—decoding each cry, moan, sneeze, and yawn, and somehow knowing what this precious child needs at each moment of the day, even before she does.

4. Somewhere along the line, realize that your marriage isn't working out. He's not the guy you thought he was, you're not the woman you thought you could be while with him, and you watch your union crumble right before your very eyes.

5. You make the decision to split up and head for divorce. You stand in a courtroom full of strangers who know nothing about you, your life, or your love for your child, and you find yourself starting to float out of your body as you wait for what comes next.

6. You're granted a percentage, far less than 100, of your ability to parent your own child. And the rest of it is given to a person you no longer love or trust.

This is parenting in pieces. *Welcome to it.*

I always say that, since the middle of the summer of 2017, I've been living a life of halves. Having a custody arrangement split straight down the middle means that only eight out of the sixteen years left of Bella's childhood at the time of my split from her dad will be mine. Half of her scrapes and boo-boos. Half of her "Mommy, look what I can do!" moments. Half of her ups. Half of her downs. Half of all of it.

Half of her entire childhood.

And that's the fuckery of co-parenting. You're now at war with—or, at best, on a very different page from—someone you once loved. You want nothing more than to protect your kids and hold them close at all times, as if your love can shield them from the way their lives are about to change. Only you can't, because your time-sharing agreement doesn't allow for it.

It hurts. There's no question about that. You grew this life in your body, after all, and now you're handing it off every few days to a man who was supposed to be by your side until death do you part. You cry after each awkward, tense exchange. You lie awake wondering how the hell you're going to deal with it forever. It takes every fiber of your being to keep you from running out the door, jumping in the car, and trailing down to your ex and the kids just to give the kids one last kiss. You're forced to have extreme self-control in a highly emotional, unnatural time of your life.

Okay, whoa. That was a lot. But that's only the bad, bad news.

Now on to the good.

You *will* survive, just like millions of other parents have.

In 2014, there were 13.4 million American parents who were sharing time with an ex, aka co-parenting.[1] Five out of six custodial parents were mothers then, and it's probably close to the same today, so, at the very least, you're not alone—no matter how lonely it feels. Now let's take you and your emotions out of the equation for a moment, because the bottom line is, co-parenting is all about the kids.

And happily, when done right, it has benefits that far outweigh the negatives.

When I first started co-parenting with Bella's dad, I was instantly transported back to my own parents' split. I came home from school on a Friday afternoon in June to my mom and grandparents sitting on my back porch, all of them in tears. I was only eight years old, but I still remember the feeling of impending doom that settled into my bowels as I walked up the driveway to join them.

"Mommy and Daddy are getting divorced," one of them told me, between my grandma's audible sobs. "Daddy has a new apartment and a new girlfriend, and you'll be with them on weekends."

Yep. Just. Like. That. It sucked.

Just a few hours later, I was in the back of my dad's Suburban with a woman I had never met, headed to an apartment I had never seen, in a town I had never heard of. Without being able to catch my breath, I was forced to adjust. Adapt. Find a way to deal with it all. And in that moment, I became resilient. (This was the good-news part, remember. Resilience is *good*.)

Now, I know that you have likely handled your own split and transition into co-parenting a little more gently. Back when I was a kid, there was no Internet to help my mom ease my brother and me into a life of back-and-forth. But no matter how gently you handle it, it still, without a doubt, will affect your children in ways that you cannot foresee.

Spoiler alert: so many of these effects lead to a whole host of AMAZING qualities that children of married people may never acquire, such as:

INCREASED SENSE OF SELF-WORTH

Here's what happens when kids are co-parented well: both of their parents suddenly get on their parenting A-game, wanting to make the most of their time with their kids and give them all they've got. This allows children to know that, no matter which home they're in or when, good things are waiting for them, making them feel worthy of love and all the greatness life has to offer. And who doesn't want a kid to grow up feeling worthy of the very best?

If you're thinking that your ex doesn't *have* an A-game, that he's worthless at parenting because of all those times he didn't get up to help you with the kids in the middle of the night, let's think logically for a second. Remember that the judge likely wouldn't have granted your ex-spouse time with the children if he were a threat to them. People who are dangerous to their children or display an inability to care for their basic human needs very often end up with supervised daytime visits before they ever graduate to overnights. Hard as it can be, you *must* have faith here.

A BETTER GRASP ON REALITY

Life is rife with loss. Most children don't experience this until later in life, when a beloved grandparent passes away or their childhood dog crosses the rainbow bridge. All of a sudden, they find themselves unable to cope, having never felt true loss before. Then there are the divorced kids, who, at some stage in their formative years, lost the life they knew and loved, and were left with no choice but to accept the reality of it. Because of this, they learn what it means to cope, self-soothe, and adapt—three skills that are undeniably crucial to happiness and success later in life.

THE WILLINGNESS TO TAKE CONTROL OVER THEIR OWN LIVES

What do you think happens when a kid watches a parent leave a situation that no longer serves them, difficult as it may be, and forge a path that leads to their own personal happiness? You guessed it. Children learn the best life lesson of all: that you have only one life, and you deserve to live it well. One of the main reasons why I didn't stay in my marriage longer than I did was because I refused to let my daughter grow up a witness to two unhappy parents going through the motions to get through the day, unable to resolve conflict, simply existing instead of living.

I knew she deserved more than that.

Whether my daughter someday resents the fact that her parents split up when she was so young is far outside my control, but what I do know is this: my daughter watched (both) her parents find their happiness after an unhappy time. You can't tell me there's a better life lesson than that.

So, as much as you might dread co-parenting, if you do it well, good things will come out of it for your child.

Okay, now back to you.

Surviving life without your kids—even for part of the time—is no easy feat. If you've gotten through the first weekend, congratulations! That's the hardest part of all. But easing yourself into a place where you can actually breathe again when your kids aren't with you takes a little time and a whole lot of perspective. A perspective shift will not only allow you to feel grateful for all of the benefits your kids will reap from a life of being co-parented, but all of the positives it'll bring to your life as well.

Here's how to shift your co-parenting perspective so that you can appreciate parenting in pieces:

RECOGNIZE THAT YOU ARE LUCKY.

Now you probably want to slam this book shut and hit me over the head with it, but give me a chance to explain. Having two parents in a child's life is a blessing and a gift, and if your ex wants to remain a positive role model and presence for the kids, then both you and your kids are lucky. Many children grow up never knowing one of their parents.

ENJOY TIME FOR YOURSELF.

The day you realize that co-parenting gives you some much-needed free time—without a hefty babysitting fee—is the day your perspective on co-parenting will change. Scroll through social media and you'll find thousands of posts from moms complaining that they never get a moment to themselves, and that they're desperate for a good night's sleep and a day of carefree nothingness.

Hello, *you* get this! When that judge granted you a life of parenting in pieces, what he was also saying was, "Queue up the Netflix shows you've been dying to watch, make plans with your girls, and invest in those luxurious silk pajamas because you've got time to yourself now, Mama!" I mentioned earlier that this alone time actually becomes the most restorative and reflective time you'll have with yourself. As soon as I was able to accept my new reality and relish the alone time, I really began to dive deep into self-improvement—emotionally, physically, and also in my business. In fact, the bulk of my success that first year of single motherhood came from all the work and strategy I'd applied to my growing marketing agency when I had my weekends free—and it made me feel so much better to know that I was increasing my earning potential. You, too, might find that, in addition to more downtime, a little extra room to focus on your career can make a huge impact.

Every so often, though, that quick scroll through social media would allow the guilt to sink in. I'd see photos of my friends at the zoo or the beach with their husbands and kids, and be reminded that I was without my child at the moment because of my own choice to end a marriage. The guilt would begin to swallow me whole. It would make me feel selfish for months to come, until I realized that after all this time, I was getting the critical alone time I needed to reconnect with myself and decompress from the incredible challenge of single parenting. I'd then reenter the arena each time I picked Bella up, with a renewed sense of energy and the patience to enjoy my child.

Co-parenting gives you the opportunity to reboot every few days, which can greatly improve your parenting skills. You get a buffer in between those "I'm so exhausted I can barely function" moments and the "Mommy, I spilled my juice on the couch again" episodes. I've always said that I'm a much better mom when I can sleep, and knowing that I get that break to sleep every couple of days helps keep me from reaching my breaking point.

KNOW THAT QUALITY IS MORE IMPORTANT THAN QUANTITY.

Kids won't remember how much time you spent with them, but they'll remember how you made them feel.

You've spent time decompressing on your days without the kids, doing things that fill up your cup, and now you're ready to love on those kids harder than ever before, each time they return to you. This is so damn beneficial for both you and your kids: the good energy, the excitement to be with them, and the fact that because you have only so much time to spend with them now, you want to make every second of it great. Many scientific studies show the quality of time a parent spends with his or her child makes a greater impact than the quantity of time. Having my daughter only 50 percent of the time has really encouraged me to make our moments together even more meaningful.

The fact that you're spending less time with your kids shouldn't be the focus. Spending that time intentionally, however, should. It means so much more to the well-being of your children and your own motherhood journey than having more time with them, if that time was spent counting the seconds until bedtime.

As you're shifting your parenting perspective, I'd like you to try implementing a few things in your life when your kids aren't with you. These are the tried-and-true strategies that I found made me feel better and that I now share with my clients. It also helps to force the perspective shift even on the days when parenting in pieces feels impossible:

HOLD YOURSELF ACCOUNTABLE FOR SOMETHING.

It's a weird feeling when you wake up one day and don't have kids pulling the covers off you, asking for a cereal bar and an iPad. It's common to feel a sudden loss of purpose. Make it a point to integrate an activity, hobby, or plan each time you're not with your children, and hold yourself accountable for it. (Something other than sitting and staring blankly into their bedrooms.) Getting into a routine, one that involves your chosen activity, hobby, or plan, keeps you busy, and busy is good!

One of the moms I worked with this year inspired me so much with her commitment to keeping her mind busy, and her body moving. When we first started working together, she confessed that she felt lost and out of touch with her true self. I asked her if she had a "thing," and she mentioned that she had been a runner for years and would run on the path along the river on the East Side of Manhattan every night after work—until her husband began giving her a hard time. "You care more about your exercise than you do our daughter," he'd say, shaming her out of that critical time to de-stress from being a full-time working mother. After our first call, I challenged her to carve out an hour of her day to throw on her sneakers and pound the pavement. Within months, she'd joined a running club where she met a whole new circle of friends, and was training for the New York City Marathon, a lifelong goal of hers.

BREAK OUT THE JOURNAL.

Yep, the trusty journal activity. Write a list of your ex-partner's strongest qualities as a parent. List why you're grateful for each one of them. For example: *One of my ex's strongest qualities is that he's always encouraging our daughter to try something new. I'm grateful for this because I'm such a creature of habit and don't find myself pushing the envelope all that often.*

Other journal prompts that help when you're away from your children:

+ Make a list of things that bring a smile to your face.

+ Make a list of places you'd like to visit with your children.

+ Make a list of the things you love about your children.

REMEMBER THAT TOMORROW IS A NEW DAY.

If you're lucky enough to wake up tomorrow, you're lucky enough to know that you're one day closer to seeing your kiddos again. Time and motherhood are both exceptional gifts.

A NOTE TO THE SINGLE MAMA WARRIORS

It's my personal belief that single moms have superhuman powers. The kind that defy all logic, push all limits, and give new meaning to the word *strong*. Single mamas, if the other parent of your children is no longer around, leaving you with no opportunity to co-parent, I want to acknowledge you, honor you, and share some really great news with you.

Though it might sometimes feel like your kids will suffer without a second parent in their lives, that's not necessarily the case. Your kids aren't doomed, and neither are you. You still have just as much opportunity to raise resilient, capable, amazing human beings.

An article I stumbled across in the *Harvard Graduate School News* back in 2015, entitled "The Science of Resilience: Why Some Children Can Thrive Despite Adversity," showed that children only need to form one healthy, secure attachment with a parent or primary caregiver in order to thrive. More specifically, the article stated:

> The experiences of the subset of children who overcome adversity and end up with unexpectedly positive life outcomes are helping to fuel a new understanding of the nature of resilience—and what can be done to build it. There's a common set of characteristics that predispose children to positive outcomes in the face of adversity, one of them being the availability of *at least one* stable, caring, and supportive relationship between a child and an adult caregiver.[2]

What's more, single moms have tapped into their superhuman badassery in recent years, dispelling the myth that single parenting is detrimental to their kids' lives. As single parenting has become more common, so has the successful single mom. In 2019, popular parenting website Mom.com published a fact that will make any single mom feel fabulous. They found "no differences in terms of parent-child relationship or child development" of children raised in a two-parent household versus a single-mother-by-choice household.

Though it might be hard, it isn't for naught. You're doing the kind of work that will no doubt result in some pretty badass kids. As badass as, hmm, let's see here: Jay-Z, Leonardo DiCaprio, Angelina Jolie, Tony Robbins, Barack Obama, and Ryan Gosling, to name a few—all raised by single mamas.

You've got this.

LONG STORY SHORT

+ Co-parenting feels like a curse, but it truly isn't—you just have to find the good!

+ Being a single parent isn't the end of the world: kids really only require one stable caregiver to thrive.

+ Co-parented kids learn some exceptional life lessons that will help them succeed as they grow.

+ You get time to reconnect with yourself and breathe yourself back to life when you're not with your kids.

+ You get time to commit to your own interests and to invest in your future.

✦ Single motherhood doesn't mean impending doom for your kids. Some of the world's most successful celebrities were raised by single moms!

JOURNAL PROMPT

What are your biggest fears about co-parenting? List them and then play devil's advocate—e.g., start with "What if everything goes wrong?" and reframe to "What if everything goes right?"

Speaking of Kids, They're Ruined Forever, Right? How Kids Process Divorce at Every Age

A in't no guilt party like a divorcing mom guilt party because a divorcing mom guilt party don't stop. Right? Well, it should. Guilt is no good for anyone, including your kids, and it's not helping you get settled in your new life. In my last four years as a co-parent, and in all of the endless research I've done along the way, I've learned a lot about what divorce *really* means for the kids involved. And it's not as bad as you think. Actually, it's probably the opposite of what every unknowing human being projects onto you when they hear about your situation. Repeat after me: *Just because someone says something doesn't mean it's true.*

Let's start with the whole "But you didn't want to stay married for the kids!?" comment. A few years back, I posted something on Instagram that went damn near viral. I was blown away by the love this post received, and realized later that the love came from women finally hearing the words they were so desperate to hear:

Your child deserves a happy mom, not a married one.

I've probably said those words about a trillion times since that post—to myself, to my clients, and to my divorcing and un-happily married friends. Because it's true. It's so damn true. Your child deserves a mom who's thriving, no matter what her marital status is. A mom who can be fully present with her kids because she isn't preoccupied with worries about her marriage. A mom who can laugh and smile and mean it, instead of holding back tears because of the last fight with her spouse.

It all comes down to who you want your child to see: the happy mom or the married mom.

That's not to say that divorce won't impact your child—everything impacts our children. But, as with anything else, there are both positive and negative impacts.

BUT DID YOU EVEN DO THE RESEARCH?

My very good friend, the beautifully brilliant early childhood expert Evelyn Mendal, LMHC, has been my ride-or-die co-parenting guru for quite some time. When I was pregnant, I attended her workshops about how to prepare for mother-hood. When Bella entered toddlerhood, I attended her work-shops that focused on healthy, mindful parenting, and how to discipline children at that wild-yet-tender age. Coinciden-tally, Evelyn separated from her ex-husband just a few months after my own separation, which afforded us the opportunity to bond and really explore what co-parenting would mean for our little girls.

"We've just totally fucked up our kids, right, Eve?" I said to her one afternoon while sobbing in a Starbucks parking lot.

"What? Mish, are you crazy? Have you even done the research on how divorce really affects kids?" she said to me, almost disappointed that I didn't know this already.

I'll admit it: I hadn't done any research on this. I had just assumed I was screwed in the parenting department. Remembering my own childhood, I imagined it would feel for Bella the way it had felt for me. But I'll be the first to admit that in the months, weeks, and days leading up to my split, I wasn't actually thinking about whether or not my impending divorce would ruin my child's life. I was more worried about getting back to a life where it didn't hurt to breathe anymore. I was desperate to feel happy instead of chronically sad and anxious.

In hindsight, I believe my body and soul knew what I preach so often to others: my child needed a happy mom, not a married mom.

But at the time, the noise from everyone around me was making me doubt myself. So I decided, as Evelyn suggested, to do the research. I went down an Internet rabbit hole of all things co-parenting, to learn exactly how I could expect my child to feel. I began seeing a therapist who specialized in co-parenting to help me get a grip. I read everything I could, committed to arming myself with knowledge.

Here's what I learned:

Yes, divorce is painful for children. The older they are, the more upset they'll become over the fact that their family will be split in two. There's no denying that the life change will take time, patience, and potentially some therapy for them to adjust to. These are short-term issues that can be worked on easily. But if you dig deeper, the research suggests that it's not really the split itself that causes long-term damage. It's the things that come after, which are completely avoidable if you're careful.

Statistically speaking, divorce affects more than one million children in the United States each year. If the actual act of getting divorced really ruined our kids so terribly, humanity would be totally and utterly devastated. Ultimately, it's our job as parents to protect and shield our kids from harm, right? Right. So, first, you need to stop looking at your divorce itself as being harmful. Hurtful for you? Yes. Absolutely. Harmful for your kids? It all depends on your outlook, how you explain it to them, and whether or not they're going to witness toxicity between you and your ex. The damage after divorce, for kids, comes when they find themselves stuck between two adults who are using them to prove a point; when they know they're being fought over; when they have to endure each parent's unhappiness about the other. Those are the things that *truly* impact children as they mature into adulthood—and therefore the things to avoid as a co-parent, no matter how much pain you're in.

Here's an age-appropriate guide to understanding how children are likely to react to the concept of divorce in the short-term sense—*NOT* the forever sense:

CHILDREN UNDER THREE:

+ Sadness

+ Fear of others, "clingy" behavior

+ Temper tantrums

+ Problems with sleeping, eating, and toilet training

+ Separation anxiety

My daughter had just turned two when my own marriage ended. I can tell you with absolute certainty that because her understanding of "family" hadn't really been developed yet, we didn't deal with sadness. Her temper tantrums at that stage—well, she was just two and already had a kick-ass independent streak. It was hard to determine if her tantrums were fueled by our divorce or by my not giving her the right spoon for her mac and cheese. She did, however, have a difficult time separating from me for a while. She loved going to see her dad—he's fun and funny and all those things—but it was tough for her to spend time away from me, and that's a natural reaction for all kids of that age. Time away from Mommy is a huge adjustment for toddlers, whether it be at school, at Grandma's house, or when the babysitter comes over so that you can run out the door for a girls' night. Kids at that age are just used to Mommy always being there.

We navigated this by making times of transition more friendly and engaging. I'd hang around with Bella and her dad for a little while, making the transition less abrupt, less like the passing of a baton. We have a Minnie and Mickey doll set. She keeps Mickey at her dad's house and I keep Minnie with me, and we made a pact to hug our dolls whenever we miss each other. They'd FaceTime when Bella missed me, which is something we still do. I always let her know that Mommy would be right there waiting for her when she got home, so she understood that there was a beginning and an end to her trips.

SCHOOL-AGED CHILDREN:

+ Moodiness (sadness, anger)
+ Temper tantrums or fighting
+ Lower school performance

✦ Worry about loyalty to both parents

✦ Strong wish for parents to get back together

I was a school-aged child when my parents split, which was not handled appropriately by any means. Psychologists today would shudder at how abrupt, contentious, and raw the whole process was for me, and how inappropriately it was explained. At the age of eight, I went from having a solid concept of family to my dad moving in with some strange woman whom I met almost instantly. It wasn't an intentional fail, though, and I chalk it up to my parents simply not knowing what they didn't know. Nonetheless, consider that a brief but concise "what not to do" when explaining divorce to a school-aged child.

The worry about loyalty was huge for me during this stage. While I knew my mom was hurting, I was having a lot of fun with my dad and this new woman, who wore entirely too much perfume and insanely revealing clothing. She bought me things and told me I was pretty and had my back when my dad was being dismissive or mean to me. This created a bit of inner turmoil, which manifested in headaches and tummy aches at school. I was in the nurse's office more than I wasn't. This was also the beginning of my long battle with anxiety.

What I needed was more clarity. More of my dad asking if I was okay. More open acknowledgment that life was totally different—and way fewer secrets and less silence. If it happened that your children's lives were rocked by a split and they were quickly introduced to the "other person," fear not. So long as you maintain open lines of communication with your children, answer their questions in an age-appropriate manner, and check in with them regularly about how they feel, they'll be okay.

I know this because I had none of this. You know better now.

ADOLESCENTS:

+ Depression, withdrawal, anger

+ Aggression

+ Engaging in risky behaviors (sex or drugs)

+ Worries about finances

+ Trouble focusing in school

Okay, well, teens are teens, right? The depression, withdrawal, and anger are likely to happen regardless of a split because of those lovely things that adolescents develop: *hormones.* Teens are weird and scary and unpredictable, and so are their emotions. It's important to know that your divorce isn't causing your preteen or teen to act this way, it's simply intensifying it. Here's what *Psychology Today* had to say about it:

> The child of divorce tends to hold on to parents more; the adolescent of divorce tends to increasingly let parents go. Over-simplifying: Divorce tends to encourage dependence in the child, and to accelerate independence in the adolescent.[1]

Children, no matter their age, will inevitably adjust to their new normal. They're amazingly resilient and adaptable, and when it comes to divorce, time really does heal all wounds. In an article about enhancing positive outcomes for children of divorce, Dr. Neil E. Farber, psychologist and professor of psychology at Arizona State University, shared that the majority of children do *not* develop significant adjustment problems that will endure throughout their lives as a result of divorce.[2] Which leads me to the positive outcomes of divorce as it relates to the children:

1. They become resilient and adaptable.
Divorce forces kids to adapt to a totally new lifestyle, almost overnight, which is a great skill to inherit for the future.

2. They become more empathetic.
This finding in my research truly made me smile. I'm a known empath, for better or for worse, and I'd like to think that this comes as a result of my own parents' divorce. A change in a family unit can make children more sympathetic to the problems of others, as it gives them a new worldview their peers may not have access to.

3. They get better quality time with their parents.
Something amazing happens for parents once they begin "sharing" their kids. They become so much more intentional and thoughtful about how they spend their time with their children, and the children absolutely reap those benefits.

WANT EMOTIONALLY HEALTHY KIDS? PARENTAL ALIENATION IS WHAT NOT TO DO

While the divorce may be inevitable, there are certain things that don't need to be, like exposing your children to conflict, forcing them to choose between parents, or making them carry the weight of your post-divorce sadness/anger/resentment. This is typically where long-lasting damage can be done. Collectively, these behaviors are known as parental alienation.

I know it's hard to bite your tongue, Mama, especially when your children are raving over how much fun they've just had with their other parent and his new flavor of the week. I know. But letting your children know how much of a slimy mother trucker you think he is will not only be a poor use of your time with your children, it may destroy their emotional well-being. This is an example of parental alienation: when one parent has more anger over the divorce than the other, using the children as instruments to attack the ex-spouse for putting the family in this new situation. It's long been reported that parents who engage in this style of alienation have narcissistic or borderline personality tendencies.[3] They have extreme reactions to even the most benign of events, and it's absurdly easy for them to feel "wronged." They're so focused on bringing the petitioning parent down to their level that they don't realize they're dragging the children down in the process.

The effects of parental alienation on children are far deeper and more long-lasting than those of divorce alone, as has been well documented since psychiatrist Richard Alan Gardner coined the term in the early 1980s. These include low self-esteem, lack of trust, depression, and substance abuse and other forms of addiction, as children lose the capacity to give and accept love from a parent. Another particularly disturbing effect is self-hatred, as kids will internalize the anger and hatred targeted toward the alienated parent. Severe guilt is also common, because children feel they're betraying one or both parents. Here's what the alienating parent never seems to understand, however: alienated children almost always end up having a conflicted relationship, or no relationship at all, with the alienating parent.[4]

What sucks the most about parental alienation is when you're forced to sit back and watch your ex engage in these behaviors with your children. If you suspect this is happening, the best thing you can do is to minimize the effects and allow your children to let their feelings out in a productive way. Therapy, if you can afford it, is always a good idea. If money is tight, ask a local support group or your family court advocate for suggestions—there may be programs in your area that can help.

LONG STORY SHORT

+ Divorce will affect the kids, but—news flash—*everything* affects kids.

+ Kids end up becoming more adaptable and resilient after this kind of transition in their lives.

+ Many of the documented effects are short-term, not long-term behaviors or predictors of what your children will be like as adults.

+ The most damaging divorce behavior for children isn't divorce itself but rather parental alienation.

JOURNAL PROMPT

Write about the last time your child(ren) displayed really impressive resilience or handled a tough situation better than you would have expected.

CHAPTER 10

Co-Parenting Life Hacks for Maintaining Consistency in Two Homes

You're vanilla. He's pistachio. You're a morning person with a strict early bedtime. He's playing video games on the couch until 3 a.m. You love to plan ahead. He's a believer in winging it. You have everything neatly scribbled in your planner. To-do lists give him hives. You believe that Jennifer Lopez is the second coming of Christ, and he just doesn't understand the importance of glowing skin and a flawless smile. You're as organized and detail-oriented as the day is long. He would lose his head if it weren't attached to his neck.

And this was before the divorce.

You're not together anymore, so these gaping holes in your relatability don't matter anymore. Phew, that solves that. Oh wait, no it doesn't. Because now, not only do you have to share kids with your polar opposite, you have no control anymore over how he parents. You start to question your own choices. *Should I have stayed just so the kids' bedtime routine doesn't go to shit? Maybe we should get back together until Susie gets through this difficult phase at school. Will Johnny ever be potty-trained with someone who's too lazy to fill him up with juice and stick him on the toilet every fifteen minutes?*

Yeah, that'll be hard. May as well just get back together. Just kidding. Please don't do that.

Here's the thing you have to wrap your pretty little head around: whether you stayed together or not, your child would be raised by people with different belief systems and different ways of doing things. Ask any one of your happily married friends right now if their husbands do things exactly how they would when it comes to the kids. Go ahead, I'll wait . . .

You see? I hate to break it to you, but these differences won't necessarily screw a child up for life. If anything, it shows children that there's always more than one way to the finish line. While there are a few key things that should stay consistent, it's important to remember that these kids are only 50 percent you, Mama, and half of them may actually prefer the way Daddy does things. But before I convince you to make a serious emotional reframe here, I want to validate your feelings. There truly is nothing harder than creating a human life that you're biologically connected to, committed to caring for, and determined to keep safe, and then handing it off to someone whom you no longer share a life, or possibly even a single value, with. It's a tough pill to swallow, but we can't have you choking on it. Instead let's focus on what you *can* do, which parts of parenting really need to line up, and which parts needn't be aligned in the slightest.

It all starts with picking your battles.

GET OVER IT

Here are some of the battles I hear women pick:

"Ugh, my ex always drops my daughter off with her hair unbrushed and crumbs from her breakfast on her chin and cheeks. It's disgusting—she looks like she's being raised in a barn! I keep fighting with him about it and it's getting me NOWHERE!"

"OMG, he buys my kid a toy every single time they're together. I don't do this. I don't believe in this. I don't want a spoiled child! I keep telling him not to, but he's not listening."

And here's one of my favorites:

"On *my* days with the kids, both of them sit down to have a snack and do their homework right after they get home from school. On *his* days, the kids tell me they're not doing their homework until after dinner!!! Every expert talks about doing homework right after school—I keep sending him articles, but I don't even think he's reading them!"

These things are as irritating as the day is long, especially if you've worked your butt off to establish routines, boundaries, and guidelines for your children that work. But they aren't the battles to pick, and here's why:

1. There are always going to be battles. And you can't win them all. You can't. And with these small things, you're draining all your energy for naught. If napkins and hairbrushes have never really been his thing in the past, they certainly won't be now. The hard truth is that he doesn't have to listen to you anymore.

2. There are more important battles to fight. Save your energy.

Your kid is okay. She's fed. She's bathed (sometimes). So, let it go, because in just a few years' time, your daughter will be able to do these things for herself. This inconsistency won't make the slightest bit of difference in the life of your child, and certainly won't hinder her ability to qualify for the swim team, get into a top-tier university, hold down a job, or form a loving partnership of her own someday.

You're probably thinking, *Small things?? These are not small things.* But they really are.

On the crumbs: He'll say that by the time he made a breakfast she actually agreed to eat, wiping her face was no longer a priority. She's fed. That's a good thing.

On the toys: He's doing what many dads think is the right thing: being the fun, indulgent parent. Annoying? Yes. Creating a toy-obsessed little monster? Probably. Guaranteeing a future of thievery and low-level misdemeanors? Absolutely not. And it doesn't mean you can't keep the same rules you always have at your own house.

On the homework: All I can hear here is that the homework got done. Homework is hard work for everyone involved, not just the kids. Count your blessings and save your energy; the articles you're sending are pointless.

Now that we've weeded out the battles not worth waging, let me be honest here. It took me years to learn the art of picking mine. There are still times my daughter tells me that her dad let her watch a movie I was saving for her teen years, sending me into a tailspin. This is where I have to stop myself from launching an all-out text war on the negative effects of PG-13 movies on five-year-olds. I don't do this anymore. It doesn't matter to me like it used to. If I've learned anything about co-parenting, it's this: if my daughter is happy, healthy, has her basic needs cared for and enjoys her time with her father, the rest is all noise not worth stressing about.

BUT DADDY LETS ME

Now that we've let the little stuff go, it's time to focus on what matters most when it comes to our kids and consistency in a co-parenting situation. According to science, dedicated researchers, and just about every co-parenting book, article, and lecture I've immersed myself in, there are two main issues that are worth fighting for. (And by fighting, I of course mean having a constructive, healthy conversation.)

Bedtime

Since the birth of your child, you've spent every single night of your life perfecting the art of the bedtime routine. You've found precisely the right time to start the process, the exact pair of pajamas that won't "feel scratchy" in the middle of the night, and the night light that perfectly keeps the Boogie Monster at bay. Having this part of your children's lives figured out not only makes your life easier; it also provides a level of comfort and stability for the kids. No matter the outcome of their day, they know exactly what is expected of them and more importantly, what to expect, come nighttime. This holds especially true once your children have to get accustomed to two different homes.

Discipline

Discipline after divorce is an area that I find my clients struggling with the most and is of great concern for all divorcing parents. Very often, I hear moms worrying about whether or not their ex-spouse will choose to discipline the kids at all, leaving them to be the "mean mom" while he becomes the fun, carefree "Disney-land dad." Or perhaps it's the opposite. You're so worried about the effects of the divorce on your children that the last thing you want to do is say no to something your ex will undoubtedly say yes to, right? I've been there. There's no better time than now to get on the same page with your ex about discipline, because it'll make both your lives a hell of a lot easier. The amazing thing about kids is that they very quickly learn exactly how to work the co-parenting system, pitting Mom and Dad against each other when it comes to discipline.

"But Daddy always lets me have candy before bed! I want to go to Daddy's house!" I heard this from my own little one way back before her dad and I got on the same page on discipline. Ouch. That stung. But there was no way I was letting her tear into a bag of Swedish Fish at 8 p.m. Kitchen's closed in my house at that time, especially for anything that will result in cavities and a sugar rush at bedtime.

"Looks like you have something to look forward to at Daddy's house" is the best answer for this, if your ex is running some kind of sugar-fueled circus at his home. Giving in to the "but Daddy lets me" bullshit will inevitably spark a domino effect of manipulation, leaving your child the victim of a discipline-less world, which, I'll have you know, doesn't make the child happier to be with you. Failure to instill a sense of discipline in children often results in kids who are unhappy, angry, and even resentful. Go figure. Discipline gives kids boundaries, and boundaries help them thrive. They know their limits, they learn respect, and once again, they know exactly what to expect from you, lowering their anxiety levels. When the discipline expectations are aligned in both households, life as a co-parent will feel much easier.

Now, how can you get your ex on the same page around

discipline? Great question. I know it seems impossible, because finding common parenting ground with someone you can barely speak to is a tough thing to do. It's not impossible, though, and if I can do it, I have faith that literally anyone else can. It all comes down to learning how to communicate the expectations around discipline to your ex from less of a "mama knows best" mentality and more of a reverse psychology, let-him-think-he's-brilliant mentality. It works. You *will* win. But it's all about strategy.

POSITIVE–NEGATIVE–POSITIVE

I first learned about the PNP sandwich effect when it came to business emails. If there was something negative or uncomfortable to communicate, using the PNP strategy was the best way to go. It works with personal relationships, too, including conversations with your ex. First, you hit 'em with a little praise, then you throw in the wrench, then wrap it all up with an oversize, glittery bow. Here's how it might go for the candy-before-bedtime situation:

> *Dear Ex,*
>
> *I'm so happy that our kids are having such a good time with you. Despite the challenges of co-parenting, you're nailing it. Also, the kids mentioned they're having candy before bed, which I know they love but isn't something I'm comfortable doing here. Do you think we can agree on doing sweet treats after school instead, so we're not stuck with crazy dental bills one day? I truly appreciate it—and thanks for sending back those sneakers. Johnny loves them!*
>
> *Chat soon!*

Instead of:

Dear Asshole,

What in the world is wrong with you? How do you ever expect our kids to learn right from wrong when they're pouring endless amounts of sugar down their throats at bedtime? These kids need discipline, and clearly you have no clue how to instill this in them. When they end up with cavities, poor sleeping habits, and a refusal to follow rules, you bet your ass I'm sticking YOU with the dental bills and meetings with the principal!

Fuckyouverymuch

TRY GETTING ON HIS LEVEL

Yes, yes, I know, he can't seem to do anything the same way you do. But that doesn't mean he isn't doing anything right. Getting on the same page doesn't have to mean it all goes your way. If there's something big-picture your ex is doing that seems to be working for your kids, agree to try it his way, and then use this as a negotiation tool. For example:

I see the kids love being able to use their phones until bedtime at your house. This isn't something I'm comfortable with at my house, but if you think it's okay and they have their homework done, I'm open to trying the same thing. Would you be willing to meet me halfway and just remove the candy from the equation?

Again, remember the importance of picking your battles. You aren't going to get everything you want.

LET YOUR KIDS LEAD

Having open and honest conversations with your kids goes a long way in regard to setting expectations of their behavior when growing up in two different homes. Talk to your kids about the rules in your home, why you have them, and what it means when they ignore them at the other parent's house. Let them know that while Daddy may allow one thing and Mommy another, the most important thing is that they maintain respect for the rules that have been put in place for them wherever they are at that moment. Think about what truly matters in the long run, and give them the chance to prove themselves—e.g., "Enjoy the candy at Dad's house, kids, just please don't forget to brush your teeth."

CHECK IN WITH EACH OTHER

No, you don't have to sit around reminiscing about better days, but you do have to remember that you're still parents together. While your obligation is no longer to each other, it *is* to the kids, and at the very least, you want to raise happy, healthy ones. Make it a point to check in with your ex on a regular basis if you can or commit to checking in with him before making any big parenting decisions. If your child is struggling with something in school, a friend, their grades, etc., this is a great time to connect over the one thing you have in common. My ex and I follow a "my co-parenting time, my decisions" lifestyle 75 percent of our lives (he's pistachio, I'm vanilla), but we naturally come together to handle bigger, more impactful situations when need be.

If all else fails and your ex uses his parenting time to purposefully go against the grain and ruffle your feathers, or manipulate the kids in his battles against you, just know this: while consistency in big parenting issues is ideal, it isn't always realistic. If you and your ex just can't get on the same page, it will not result in your children morphing into feral animals.

LONG STORY SHORT

✦ Maintaining consistency in two homes means getting clear on what really matters.

✦ Let the little stuff go.

✦ Your child won't end up a felon if your co-parent overindulges him.

✦ Bedtime and discipline are two core issues to try to come together on.

✦ Coming together might mean sacrificing some of your beliefs and preferences.

✦ Not being able to come together won't mean the end of the world for your child.

JOURNAL PROMPT

Make a list of your "co-parenting nonnegotiables" and then cross off the ones not worth fighting for. Circle your top three and remind yourself to focus on those and those only.

CHAPTER 11

The Parenting-Plan Secrets No One Has Told You About

I'm eternally in a rush. Straight to the finish line is how I operate, always looking for shortcuts. I'm a "first to arrive at the party, first one to leave" kinda gal. So naturally, I've never been the girl who takes the time to read directions, the fine print on the contract, or the terms and conditions—ever. In fact, we've got more half-finished Lego play sets sitting around Bella's playroom than I care to admit, because, well, have you seen those direction booklets? This is one of my most toxic traits, and I fully recognize that. In true Michelle style, when first meeting with my divorce attorney and being asked if I understood the details of a standard parenting plan, I naturally said yes, and quite possibly believed it. I never asked a single question about it, until I learned a few things the hard way (totally on-brand, I know).

Shortly after this meeting with my attorney, my ex-husband and I started co-parenting Bella. We didn't have many rules in place other than a temporary time-sharing agreement. My anxiety about letting her leave my sight for overnight visits at her dad's house was through the roof.

Back then, the only thing I understood was that whatever

parenting plan we chose, it would cut my motherhood journey in half. Fifty percent. Eight years instead of sixteen. What else was there to know?

LEARNING THE HARD WAY

One sweltering Sunday in June, I woke up late by mom standards—around 9 a.m. I was rested and relaxed until I remembered it was my least favorite day of the year: Father's Day. Of all 365 days in the calendar year, this is the one that made my blood boil. I didn't have a father to honor, after all, and each "Daddy's girl" caption that appeared under every photo on my Facebook feed drove me insane with jealousy. *These are grown women, for god's sake*, I'd think. *Get a life.* (Obviously, those were my salty daddy issues talking.)

Anyway, as if Father's Day couldn't make me more miserable, I was now separated. So now not only was I fatherless on Father's Day, I was without a husband, and thanks to co-parenting, I was also without my child. My heart ached for Bella more than usual. I couldn't wait to hear from her, even if just for a moment. I tried to distract myself, picking up my journal to let out some emotions, when another fatherless friend texted and asked if I wanted to go to brunch. *Hell yes*, I thought, *the perfect distraction*.

I got myself dressed and ready, leaving my phone in the other room on purpose—you know, that thing you do when you're willing with all your might for someone to call you. *Maybe if I walk away from it for a second, it'll ring*, I told myself. It didn't.

I got in the car and made an effort to drive the five minutes to our brunch spot at a slower-than-usual speed, hoping I'd get a phone call before arriving at my destination. It was almost 10 a.m. at this point, and I knew there was no way I was going to be able to enjoy brunch without having heard from Bella. *Screw it, I'll just call them*, I thought.

After far too many rings, I reached my ex's voice mail, which sent chills up my spine. No answer. My mind raced. My heart did too. I was sweaty and overwhelmed with anxious thoughts. Did Bella's father not wake up? Did he die in his sleep? Did he forget to put the child safety lock on the front door? Did Bella wander out of his first-floor apartment into oncoming traffic wearing nothing but a diaper? Speaking of diapers, did she need a diaper change?

My thoughts instantly hopped aboard the hot-mess express that morning, and were plowing full speed toward a brick wall.

I arrived at brunch in a panic. I was convinced something terrible had happened. "Call again," my friend insisted, before she went back to talking about something completely irrelevant to my current state of existence. I called again. And again. And probably a hundred more times.

"Relax. I'm sure they're fine," my friend said unconvincingly as my eggs sat cold and untouched on the table in front of me. She was rattling off something about the guy she hadn't heard from since their last date, pressing me for my thoughts on whether or not he'd call again, until I couldn't take it anymore. I threw some cash on the table, made a beeline for the door, jumped back in my car, and sped like a bat out of hell to my ex's apartment.

I was just reaching his exit when my phone rang. It was him. "What is wrong with you?" he asked. "What's the emergency?" All I could do to try to justify my thirty-plus phone calls to him that morning was cry. "You need to calm down," he said. "Bella must have been playing with my phone and left it under my bed. I couldn't find it all morning. She's fine. We're fine. Bella, say hi to Mommy."

He was right. I needed to calm down. This was me—all me. I got off at the exit and pulled into a gas station parking lot. I was sobbing uncontrollably. Panic, shame, and sheer relief overtook my body, leaving me trembling in the front seat of my Jeep. I knew I was being crazy. How could I live like this? How could I spend each weekend in distress until I heard from her? Who can handle this kind of existence?

The next day, I called my lawyer—and my therapist, too, if I'm being honest. I told my lawyer the story and insisted I couldn't do this co-parenting thing. I told her I wasn't cut out for it, and that we needed to do something before this went any further. Deep down, I knew Bella's dad would never really withhold calls from me. It was the fact that I couldn't get in touch with them when I needed to that made me feel so out of control, so disheartened. My lawyer reminded me that I had told her I was steadfastly in favor of co-parenting. That I was committed to helping Bella have a loving relationship with her father. And she told me that we could add mandatory phone calls to the parenting plan.

"Add mandatory phone calls to the parenting plan?" I asked, almost in shock that this could even be a thing.

"We've only just started crafting this thing," my lawyer reminded me. "We can essentially ask for whatever it is you want. Think of it as a blank canvas."

This is when I finally opened up the PDF in my in-box labeled "sample parenting plan" and got to work. From that day on, whenever she was at her dad's, Bella FaceTimed me twice a day: once in the morning and once before bed.

LIKE PICASSO, BUT WITH WORDS

I've learned a lot about parenting plans since my dramatic Father's Day brunch. I've learned even more about them since diving deep into my coaching practice and working with women to help them understand their own parenting plan desires. Look, I'm not a lawyer, and unless you are, it can be hard to understand all your options when you're just trying to push your divorce over the finish line.

Essentially, a parenting plan is a standard business contract that requires unique and personalized customization from both parents involved to make it a true masterpiece. It will outline the rest of your life as a parent, and it'll be up to you to grab the brush and paint to create the perfect work of art. You have to think of yourself as a Picasso of sorts, but with a pen, and take your sweet time thinking things through. Rushed, emotionally driven decisions do not a good parenting plan make. Take it from me.

Below are the basic parenting plan items you need to think through, carefully, before you just sign off on any old thing to avoid a prolonged battle. I see far too many women jump to an answer, any answer, if it means getting the paperwork signed more quickly. NEWS FLASH: There are no prizes for speed in this situation. Pay attention to every detail, because they will inevitably shape the way you live your life.

Right of First Refusal

The right of first refusal is a clause that says that the parent who has custody of the kids has to offer parenting time to the non-custodial parent any time the custodial parent cannot watch the children, rather than seeking a babysitter first.

If I had a dollar for every client who has never even heard of this clause in their parenting plan, I'd be wealthier than the lawyers writing them. Thankfully, my lawyer explained it to me in very careful layman's terms, after I glossed over the question without giving it any thought because I was so fixated on some of my ex's other demands for the plan. This isn't one you'll want to gloss over, and here's why.

Imagine you're me, circa 2017. After a painful separation, you meet the man of your dreams. He has a job that requires him to attend a lot of galas, fundraisers, and cocktail hours. It's exciting, and you can't wait to get dressed up and be the lady on his arm. But there's an issue: most of these events fall on the nights that you have your children with you. Well, if you want to attend these events and you haven't addressed the right of first refusal carefully and with extreme detail in your parenting plan, you can kiss your nights with the kids goodbye, because it's your ex's right to have them if you're not available to be with the kids on your time. This may sound like a great free babysitting service, but what it really means is that you'll be losing an entire night with your children each time you have plans. You will have to trade those nights you go out for *other* nights when you don't.

The answer is to do what my lawyer advised me to do, which was to extend the window of time for which you can hire a babysitter, call Grandma over to watch the kids, or let them go on a playdate. For me, it was seven hours instead of the standard two to three hours. This meant that I had up to seven hours to go and do what I needed to do on my parenting time before having to call in my ex and beg for him to switch a night with me. We decided on this number after my lawyer broke down the time frame of a typical night out in Miami:

Up to one hour to get to the event destination +

A one-hour cocktail party followed by a four-hour reception +

An infuriatingly long valet line +

An hour to get home =

7 hours.

BRILLIANT, I remember thinking. I never would have come up with this on my own.

The modification in the clause helped tremendously, because it allowed me to kiss my baby good night, put her to sleep, leave the babysitter with a pizza, enjoy my night with my guy, and still be able to wake up in the morning to the kisses and cuddles from my girl—without her even knowing I was gone. I made a point to always be the one to put her to bed on my nights, even if it meant showing up late to a cocktail hour.

Note that this clause goes both ways, though. When you set up your right of first refusal to give you some flexibility in your personal life, it gives your ex the same exact opportunity. Think this through carefully if having your child spend time with a sitter isn't your first choice.

Childcare

Speaking of sitters, did you know you have the right to approve or disapprove of the childcare choices your ex makes (and vice versa)? If it looks like sitters, nannies, or childcare persons of any kind will be making their way into your child's life at your ex's home, it may be wise to add to your parenting plan that you'd like to have a say in who's hired when you aren't around. This helps to put even the most anxious of mamas' minds at ease (and by "the most anxious of mamas" I mean me, obviously).

Holidays and Birthdays

Show me the parent who doesn't mind losing time with their child on the holidays or for a birthday, and I'll show you a big fat liar. When you sit down to negotiate this part of your parenting plan, you'll be offered the standard even/odd-year breakdown, such as, Mom has the kids for the holidays in even years and Dad has them in odd years. This is straight-up bullshit, in my opinion, because this kind of split doesn't take into account that some holidays are celebrated for more than one day. It doesn't take into account that one party's extended family may be coming into town on the other parent's year to have the kids, preventing them from holiday hugs or gift exchanges. This is a model worth challenging, and here are some creative ways to Picasso the holiday and birthday section of your parenting plans:

Instead of, let's say, doing the even/odd-year thing for Christmas as a whole, give some thought into splitting the holiday in half each year. This would mean that one year, Mom has Christmas Eve into Christmas morning, then drops the kids off at Dad's by 10 a.m., allowing him to have Christmas Day and Christmas dinner with the kids. The next year, that schedule would swap. This means the kids get to see *both* their parents on the most exciting holiday of the year, and everyone wins.

Now, don't kill me, but I typically share a rather unpopular opinion when it comes to our children's birthdays. I've been dragged by plenty of unkind Instagram followers for this opinion, fielding "omg she's crazy" comments each time I share it.

To which I respond, "I'm not crazy, I'm child-focused when it comes to co-parenting."

My "crazy" suggestion? If you're able to, spend your children's birthdays together, with your ex, no matter how much you wish he'd get sucked up into the vacuum of space and eaten alive by a black hole. This is one of the most child-centered co-parenting decisions you can make, because you're giving your children the gift of being with *both* of the humans who created them. Your friends and family may not understand this generous decision. They'll say, "How could you possibly spend another second with him?"

"It's for the kids," you'll say, as you lay your head down that night knowing you did the right thing.

The flip side:

If your child is aware of high stress between you and your and ex, you don't want that stress to spoil a birthday. You do what's right for your child that year, and readdress it the following year.

The other option is that your child has *two* birthday parties. That's right. One parent can throw the "big" one this year, while the other parent can do something totally different on a smaller scale—or a special birthday outing, rather than a full-fledged party—the day before or after.

Phone Calls

I've heard of some wild phone call clauses in some parenting plans: once per weekend, twice in a week, only if the child asks. I'm not okay with any of these, but if you are, more power to you. I highly recommend the two-call-per-day clause, especially when children are super young, because it keeps you connected to your children, and them to you. And in my mind, this level of contact is incredibly important for younger kids, who have little concept of time and may miss you without having a way to express it.

The flip side:

Having your ex call twice a day when it's your turn to have the kid may disrupt your time together. He's asking too many questions about what is "going on at Mommy's house." Maybe you want the phone calls to be limited to two five-minute calls per day or one ten-minute call per day. This depends on the age of your child. Don't forget, your ex will most likely be listening in on everything that's said. As the children get older, you can demand that the conversations become private.

Ultimate Decision-Making Authority

Here's something I bet you didn't know: you can share custody with an ex-spouse yet still maintain ultimate decision-making authority. Typically, the presumption under the law is that the responsibility of parenting will be shared, but often, in the best interest of the child, one parent may make some or all of the decisions.

I wouldn't expect your ex to agree to this automatically, as it's typically something that's decided in court, but if you feel that you would be better equipped to make certain decisions for your child (such as about schooling) it may be worth fighting for. This is definitely something to explore with your lawyer.

Other Issues to Not Gloss Over

+ Travel—How much notice will you want to receive/give of any travel plans involving the children?

✦ Documents—Which of you will hold on to important documents belonging to the children, including passports and birth certificates?

✦ Doctor Appointments—Do you want to have to get permission from your ex for each medical visit your child has? Do you want your ex to get permission from you?

✦ Exchanges—Do you want your ex inside your home when he comes to pick up the kids? For how long? Would it be easier to meet in a neutral location? Or will that become logistically complicated?

Be 400 Percent Sure

You know what I did with my parenting plan that I wish I hadn't done? I rushed it. I rushed it without really thinking about the future. I rushed it because I wanted to get it over with. I rushed it because every email exchange between my lawyer and his threw my anxiety over the edge. I rushed it without realizing that modifying a parenting plan* later on down the road can make the initial divorce process look like a cakewalk, at least in the state of Florida. (Which is a good reminder: definitely ask your lawyer about your state's specific requirements on all counts.)

Take it from me: think things through. I know you want it over and done with. I *know*. I know you're worried about the here and now, and you're ready to move on with your damn life without spending another small fortune on legal fees. But a rushed parenting plan will come back to bite you in your newly

---

* At least under Florida law, the standard of proof to modify a parenting plan is greater than that to establish the original parenting plan.

single ass, I can promise you this. Take your time, play out every possible scenario in your head a million times, and be 400 percent sure that you're okay with what you're signing. It's as good as being written in stone.

LONG STORY SHORT

+ This is one area of your life where you won't want to learn things the hard way.

+ Don't rush your decision-making process for any items on the parenting plan; they'll all be of some importance at one point or another.

+ Ask questions if you don't understand what is being presented/offered/asked of you.

+ Your parenting plan is your co-parenting bible. Write it carefully.

JOURNAL PROMPT

Take a look at your parenting plan, or if you don't have one yet, Google a sample plan for the state that you live in. Read it carefully and write down any questions you have about any areas of the plan that confuse you. If you have a plan, write down the things you wish you could change. You may decide they're worth fighting for.

CHAPTER 12

My Ex Hates Me.
Will His Anger Ever Go Away?

The marriage was not good. It was less than good. It was as comforting as wet sand in your underpants. He didn't give you the love you needed, let alone any respect or sense of security. You felt invisible to your spouse. Your attempts to connect, seek validation, or feel like the woman he once loved and desired fell on deaf ears, blind eyes, and a blackened heart. You were convinced that he didn't have a shred of love for you left in his body. His emotional absence was crippling, and you were ready to stand in the shoes he couldn't fill, ready to give yourself the love you so deserved. You were ready for comfort and ease, and if those were impossible with him around, you were fully prepared to go find them yourself.

Leaving felt like the only way out of this world of neglect and pain. You were sure he wouldn't miss you when you were gone. In fact, you were convinced he'd barely even notice once he had the freedom to live the life he was dying to live. So you did the hard thing. You left this marriage in search of what you truly deserved. You spent months, years even, gathering the courage to make this change. You chose bravery. You chose *you*.

And now he's making your life miserable because of it. You truly believe that he hates you, or at least he's acting like he does, and it's making your life hell. It's causing you to second-guess your choices, your bravery, and your strength. When someone projects all that hate onto you, it's naturally going to be hard to muster what you need to love about yourself.

SERENITY PRAYER

In all my work with divorcing women, there's one woman in particular whose ex-husband will forever go down in the history of my mind as the world's worst. He spent years physically abusing her in their marriage. He cheated on her left and right, flaunting it in her face. He made well over seven figures a year in real estate, yet made her beg for money to buy groceries. It took everything she had to leave him so that she and her four-year-old child could have a chance to live a normal life. She moved in with an aunt who helped her get back on her feet. She thought this would finally be the end of her long nightmare.

Boy, was she wrong. The fact that she dared to leave him sparked a hate within him that only seemed to grow stronger. By the time she reached out to me, she was two-and-a-half years into their divorce battle and feeling completely defeated.

"I can't co-parent with a man like this," she sobbed. "Will his anger ever go away?"

Well, while I don't have a crystal ball or the ability to predict the future, I can confidently say this: whether your ex's anger goes away or not isn't the issue. You can't control him or his behavior, as you've learned by the fact that you needed to divorce him to reclaim your life. You have one job now, and it has nothing to do with him. You have to learn how to build a wall around you so thick that his anger and hate cannot penetrate—so that it reflects off you and turns the blinding light of his rage right back onto him.

It all comes down to that serenity prayer that your mom, aunt, or grandmother might have had hanging on her fridge when you were a kid:

> God grant me the serenity
> To accept the things I cannot change;
> Courage to change the things I can;
> And wisdom to know the difference.

Yes, you have to accept his hate. Accept it as a flaw within himself that he cannot fix, and that you can't either. Accept it as the not-so-glamorous parting gift you have been handed on your way out the door of this unhappy, unhealthy marriage. And then turn the focus on yourself, because you have to be strong as a mother to withstand the roller coaster of co-parenting and life after divorce with a high-conflict ex.

You have to start looking at your ex's behavior as nothing more than rain at the beach. You know: those days where you're finally enjoying a relaxing day at the beach, toes deep in the sand, kids playing happily with their buckets and pails, your mind far away from the current reality of your life. Out of nowhere, a clap of thunder jolts you back from your brief respite. You scramble to gather your belongings, throw some clothes on the kids, and run for cover. You shake off the sand, do what you can to keep the kids from being scared, and wait for the storm to pass. You don't stand on your beach chair and begin shouting obscenities at each clap of thunder in hope it'll back down, do you? No, you don't do this, because you know it wouldn't work. Also, you don't want to scare the kids even more than they already are. The same goes for each storm your ex brings your way.

Below are some strategies that can help you take cover, shield yourself from the storm, and show that angry sky that he simply cannot ruin your day at the beach.

BOUNDARIES ARE A DIVORCING MOM'S BEST FRIEND

If you know me via Instagram, attend my workshops, or have ever heard me open my mouth, for that matter, you know that I can't stress enough the importance of setting boundaries—especially with a high-conflict ex. Why? Because boundaries are the only way to afford yourself the three most necessary P's of moving on: peace, protection, and power. Setting boundaries isn't about telling your ex what to do or how to do it, it's simply sending a message about what you will and won't tolerate. It brings you peace in the sense that it stops you from fighting back. Boundaries protect your energy because they stop you from being swept up in negative energy. They help you take your power back, because they serve as your metaphorical bodyguard, one that won't allow nonsense to penetrate your vibe any longer.

There are three types of boundaries that need to be addressed and implemented in a high-conflict co-parenting situation: emotional, tactical, and physical.

Emotional Boundaries

Emotional boundaries serve to protect your spirit from getting sucked into his drama. Think of your emotions as an egg and the boundaries as an egg carton. Without the carton, what would happen to the egg after the slightest jolt? A potential crack in the shell, or if the jolt hit hard, total destruction, right? This is why emotional boundaries are essential, especially when you're at your most vulnerable after a divorce. You need that metaphorical Styrofoam carton sealed shut around you, so that no matter which way your ex tries to jolt you, your shell stays nice, smooth, and without the possibility of a crack.

Here are three examples:

1. No response is a response.

You don't have to respond to things that don't need a response. When he comes digging for information about your personal life, begins criticizing you and your parenting skills, directs blame at you for things that aren't your fault, you'll naturally feel compelled to answer, stand up for yourself, and have the last word. Stop. There's no need. It's like screaming into the wind, a giant waste of good energy. Not responding to his attempts to pull you into his hate and anger will send a clear and concise message of "I'm not stepping into the ring just because you want to box."

2. Treat your relationship like a business.

Your relationship is no longer one based on emotion (although you wouldn't know that based on how he's behaving), but rather, one focused solely on the important business of co-parenting children together. If there needs to be communication on your end or in response to him, it shouldn't be about anything other than the kids. Take the emotional language and blame out of your questions and responses. For example, instead of "I really need you to make more of an effort to get the kids to school on time. It's really hurtful to know that you just don't seem to care about doing anything right," try "Per the parenting plan, please ensure the children arrive at school on time."

3. Keep your guard up.

I'll admit, I've ignored this important rule of emotional boundary-setting more than once. It's hard to abide by this boundary when you're aching for a normal, amicable co-parenting relationship. You may find that after months and months of feeling like your ex is sticking pins and needles into a voodoo doll he's crafted in your likeness, he'll begin to treat you like a friend. You'll start to have normal conversations, talk about how wonderful your child is, and forget that just yesterday, his eyes basically burned and bled at the sight of you. You'll get giddy at the thought of finally having turned a corner. Then, right when you're ready to pat yourself on the back for turning a high-conflict relationship peaceful, you'll hear the rumblings of thunder off in the distance again, and be reminded why you can never let your guard down. Can this unevenness level out at some point? Absolutely; time always has a way of working its wonders. But until it does, best to keep yourself safe emotionally just in case.

Tactical Boundaries

Tactical boundaries are about using tools or processes to protect yourself. One way to establish a key tactical boundary is to pick one form of communication and stick to it. Your ex no longer reserves the right to call, text, email, send smoke signals, or leave notes on your windshield. If he's high-conflict and gets his kicks from constantly badgering you, my advice is to always use a co-parenting communication app. Conversations held on these platforms are admissible in court, and cannot be manipulated or deleted. If your ex won't use one of these apps, email is best. Limiting the communication to one method will help keep the notifications to a minimum, and messages will be easy to find should you ever need to present this information to your attorney.

These days, we've got shortcuts and loopholes and tech solutions up the wazoo. We're adjusting the temperatures inside our homes from work. We're talking to robots in the cloud about some of life's most complex questions, and then we're telling them to play some '90s hip-hop classics. My husband not only controls what's happening in the barbeque from inside the house, he also just found a way to increase the strength of our plug-in air freshener from. his. PHONE.

So, don't let your ex tell you there's no "easy" button for co-parenting.

Yes, There IS an App for That

A few years ago, Bella's dad shared the name of "this app thing" for co-parents that he thought we should try out. Now, I think this goes without saying, but my first thought was, *How in the hell is an app going to help?*

"It's got a messaging feature," he said.

Great—so does my phone, my Instagram, my Facebook, and my Gmail account, I thought.

"It also has a place for us to track our expenses and how much we owe each other," he continued.

Okay, now he had my attention.

"And we can put our days with Bella into the shared calendar. If either of us needs to switch a day, we can just request it on the app without having to talk to each other."

"Well, with that, good sir, you've got yourself a deal."

I couldn't believe I had never heard of this kind of magic co-parenting sorcery before. I'm the type of woman who prides herself on staying up to date on the latest and greatest ways to simplify my life: hello, Amazon Prime for all things. With a rush of excitement and a tinge of jealousy for not having heard of this app first, I downloaded it and got to work on incorporating all of its functions into my day-to-day life. Ironically, it wasn't long before I became connected with the app on a more personal level: the company took me on to help market it and I became a key educator for their co-parenting courses.

Here's why I loved the app so much: it removed the confrontation from uncomfortable situations, the kind that would normally escalate tensions between us. I've seen this transformation happen time and again with my clients, many of whom start out telling me, "We will *never* be able to communicate without fighting."

One client, who I'll call Jane, came to me one day exasperated. "I can't even ask him what time he's dropping the kids off without him launching into an all-out attack on me," she said. "It's borderline abusive." She had me take a look at her messages from her ex—emails, texts, even a scribbled note he'd left in their child's backpack. He had way too much access to her at all times for all the wrong reasons. And she was right: his comments were completely abusive, out of line, and had nothing to do with their children.

"You need to limit your conversations to one place and keep it child-focused," I said. "The only way to get him to fall in line with this is by using a co-parenting app."

"He'll never go for it," she insisted.

But to our surprise, he did. He not only used it, he also stopped belittling her because he knew that the text threads in this app could be reviewed by their judge. The tension between them eased, and so did her anxiety around communicating with him. Using the app didn't eliminate his anger or her pain, but it did take the drama out of the simple conversations they needed to have about their kids.

It worked like this for me too. If I wanted to request to switch a night with Bella's father for whatever reason, the app gave me the ability to do so without having to call, text, or explain myself.

If I didn't want to have to continually nag him to remind him about expenses he owed me and vice versa, I simply added it to the list in the expense tracker feature of the app.

And being able to text through the app was gold too. The text threads—should you find yourself back in front of a judge for any post-judgment issues—cannot be manipulated, deleted, etc. They're all right there, and the court is allowed to have access to them.

There are many other apps out there like this one, but all have the same goal: making co-parenting easier. Just do a quick Google search of the best co-parenting apps and you're bound to find one tailored for you, your ex, and your current co-parenting challenges. The trick is knowing when to call in this co-parenting lifeline.

Not sure if you need one? There *are* some telltale signs that it's time to download a co-parenting app:

1. Your ex is in constant contact with you.
If your ex is reaching out multiple times a day, through multiple platforms, and it's starting to feel invasive and over-bearing, it's time for a co-parenting app.

2. Your ex harasses/threatens you via text and you'll need to go back to court.

With regular texting, conversations can be deleted. With an app, nothing can be deleted. That means if you end up in court again for whatever reason, the judge will get a clear picture of what is happening—and the threat of that will likely keep your ex on his best behavior, at least in print.

3. One or both of you keeps forgetting your co-parenting days.

Yes, this really does happen. You know, the whole "But I told you I couldn't have her this day—I have an important work event," followed by the "You never told me that—you're crazy!" A calendar feature will save you.

4. You have a hard time keeping track of who owes each other money.

Whether you're splitting day-to-day costs for your kids or have settled on splitting big-ticket items like braces, insurance, and school tuition, these things get complicated quickly. If you're anything like me, you tell yourself that you'll write everything down and save receipts, but that never, ever happens. Then you're left wracking your brain for what you might have spent last month, get frustrated, and don't even bother asking for reimbursement. Your little app will allow you to keep track of these things and, if you're using an app, your ex will get an alert each time you add something new to the list.

5. You just can't seem to have a productive conversation without fighting.

If each attempt one of you makes to talk to the other about even the most benign of subjects turns into an all-out attack, use an app. You'll thank me later.

Physical Boundaries

Physical boundaries are crucial. It will be damn near impossible to move on when you and your ex find yourselves in the same physical space time after time. Think of these as the moat around your castle—feel free to fill that moat with alligators if need be.

Physical boundaries protect you from certain tricky co-parenting situations, like exchanges of the children. In many cases, there are co-parents who aren't ready to be in one another's space. It could be that one parent is nervous about having the other parent in their home, or they aren't ready to enter the ex-spouse's new home for one reason or another. A woman I know had an ex-husband who, when he came to pick up the kids, would often invite himself inside, make himself a sandwich, and sit at the kitchen table they once shared as a couple. This would make her skin crawl. He was unpredictable in the sense that some days he was friendly and amicable, and other days he would refuse to leave when it was time. She even once found him snooping through her mail. Fortunately, I was able to help this client draw an important line in the sand that clearly specified how exchanges were to happen from that moment on. Her ex waited in the car as Mom got the kids ready to go and walked them outside. She had to add this clause to her parenting plan in order to enforce it, but found it well worth the effort to do so.

Speaking of physical boundaries, one thing not to accept or

ignore as you're learning to cope with your ex's emotional hate? Physical abuse. If you suffered physical abuse at the hands of your partner or soon-to-be ex, this isn't the kind of behavior you can brush under the rug and assume will dissipate. This is absolutely an issue to discuss with your attorney, especially if you believe your children could be in harm's way when alone with him. There are many ways to allow your ex to have time with the children in a safe, controlled environment while still ensuring their physical safety is a top priority. Don't shy away from bringing this up!

JUST A REMINDER: YOUR KIDS ARE WATCHING

If all else fails, and the weight of your ex's anger seems to pull you in time and time again, remember this one thing: your kids are watching. Whether your ex is outwardly sharing his pain and anger with the kids or they're just feeling a tension palpable even to the most innocent of bystanders, it's there, like a big ol' pink elephant standing in the middle of your house and his. One angry parent? Okay, we can work around this. TWO angry parents? No way, Mama. Your kids need safe harbor, which is exactly why you can't lose your cool and composure and stoop to the angry man's level. You owe this level of calm to your children, and as they grow, they'll be so damn proud to have had a mom that taught them the important lessons of standing tall and strong in the face of even the ugliest storms, and never letting the storm get the best of her.

LONG STORY SHORT

✦ Your ex's anger is his problem, not yours.

✦ You cannot control how your ex feels no matter how hard you try.

✦ You can control how you respond to his anger.

✦ Boundaries will save you. Set them and stick to them.

✦ Your children need only ONE stable parent to thrive.

✦ Physical abuse of any kind must be addressed with a legal or mental health professional.

JOURNAL PROMPT

What are some boundaries you want to start enforcing with your ex to keep his emotions out of your new mindset?

CHAPTER 13

I Hate My Ex.
Will My Anger Ever Go Away?

There's no pain quite like watching the person you once walked down the aisle with walk out the door to start a whole new life without you. I've learned this from watching my friends' marriages fall apart. I've learned this from working with clients whose husbands up and left them in search of something or someone else. I learned this after watching my dad get caught with another woman and choose her, only to leave my mom alone with two young children. The pain is brutal, and my heart breaks for all the women who are forced to put their pain aside in order to co-parent with the person who destroyed them emotionally.

But that's exactly what it takes—putting your pain aside.

Whether you find yourself in this new stage of uncoupling because of infidelity or just because you or your ex had a change of heart, it's perfectly reasonable that you feel filled with anger, pain, and hate. This person has now turned your world completely upside down, shaken it up with no warning, and left you to pick up the broken pieces all on your own. The hate becomes more and more palpable with each passing day, especially if he seems to be living his life unbothered, as you sob uncontrollably whenever you have the opportunity.

THE DEEPER THE LOVE, THE DEEPER THE HATE

"How could I hate someone that I loved so much?" I've been asked by clients and friends alike. "He was my world. I did everything for him. I was so in love with him."

"Hate is normal," I would say. "It's a perfectly natural part of this process."

Hate is a by-product of love, I've learned, in the sense that the deeper you love someone, the deeper you can hate that person. The two emotions mirror one another. *Psychology Today* once reported on a study by Zeki & Romaya (2008) that looked at people's brains while viewing images of the faces of people they either loved or hated.[1] The results revealed that some of the same brain areas were activated in the two conditions. One of those areas is the insular—a brain region that determines the intensity of an emotion and how strongly we take it to be associated with what we perceive (in this case, the person). The insular doesn't determine whether the emotion is positive or negative. Hate and love thus both seem to be involved in the neural processing of what is sometimes referred to as the arousal effect of emotion (and I don't mean the panties-around-your-ankles kind of arousal). Thus, an emotion with a high arousal effect can quickly turn from positive (love) to negative (hate).

I know you've heard this famous quote before: *Hate is like drinking poison and expecting someone else to die,* and it's true. Because when you carry your hate into your co-parenting life, it very often hurts your kids most of all. The more time you spend with these negative feelings, the more likely it is that they'll rub off on the kids, and the less likely it is that you'll be able to move on in a healthy way. And we need you to move on, Mama—you deserve that. Plus, the best revenge is living a really great freakin' life.

Learning to let go of hate and resentment is a process that takes time and requires patience. It doesn't happen overnight. Hate festers if you let it, and you have to find ways to replace that hate with love before it eats you alive.

Before we get into *how* to release the bitter hate and resentment you understandably hold in your heart, let's focus on *why* you need to let that shit go.

It's About You

Moving on after a marriage is climbing one hell of a mountain. You need strength, energy, and a positive outlook in order to start your trek to the summit. Not to mention, holding onto hate is bad for your health—literally. The American Heart Association has reported higher rates of heart disease among people with intense feelings of anger. You need to take care of you right now in order to take care of your children and to create a happier, more fulfilling future.

It's About Your Children

Maybe (hopefully) you don't express your hate for your spouse in front of your children, but I promise you, they can still feel it. Kids are wildly intuitive. Be mindful of the fact that you're not just communicating with words around your ex: kids can read your body language, feel the tension, and study your expressions without your noticing. Ask yourself this: *Do I love my children more than I hate my ex?* I'm pretty sure I know the answer to this one, so that should tell you all you need to know about how important it is to let the hate go.

Stop Picking at That Scab

Think of the last time you woke up with that dreaded sense of "Ugh, why me? I hate that stupid man so much." How did the rest of your day go? Not well, I imagine. You probably then wanted to curse out the poor Starbucks barista who messed up your coffee order, which then bled into your wanting to rip your friend a new one after she canceled your lunch date at the last minute, and then wanting to curse out the sweet old lady who took the parking spot you were gunning for at the supermarket. It's like a wound that won't stop bleeding. Carrying such negative emotions around in your heart all day will no doubt seep out into all other areas of your life. You'll be more short-tempered, less able to focus on your work or what you enjoy doing. Needless to say, this is counterproductive for moving on.

LET THAT SHIT GO

Ladies, what are we doing?
   Letting go of hate.
   Why?
   Because we deserve happy lives.
   When?
   ASAP, if not sooner.
   How?
   Oh, shit; that's the hard part.
   Actually, the truth is, letting go of hate and resentment is

one of the most powerful ways to start turning your lemons into lemonade. It begins with making a choice and standing behind it. It begins and ends with you.

Own It
Don't feel guilty about your feelings of anger, resentment, and hate. They're natural, although they might feel foreign if you have lived your life up until this point as a generally happy, loving, and kind human being. Own and acknowledge that it's okay to feel them. Making peace with even the ugliest feelings is a step in the right direction—you can't let go of something until you've accepted the role it plays in your life.

Exorcise It
Maybe not with green projectile vomit and seizure-like contortions, but you *will* have to exorcise these demons. Because that's exactly what feelings of anger and hate are: demons that will try to control every part of your life and take all of the happiness out of it. Find a safe way to express your hate so that you can release it from your body. No, I'm not suggesting you take a can of red spray paint to your ex's car to let everyone know he's a cheating asshole. I'm talking about a more productive, less-likely-to-get-you-arrested type of expression:

Writing.

Take your journal, a piece of scrap paper, or a photo of your ex and a pen. Write a letter that says exactly how you're feeling, right at this very moment, detailing every inch of your ugliest thoughts. Then fold it up, put it in a drawer, and do this again each time those thoughts start to take over your body and mind. After each writing session, make it a point to do something you love, or something that will get your endorphins flowing. Go for a walk, play with your kids, take a nap if the task exhausted you. And make this a habit.

Depersonalize It

What if I told you that your ex's actions had absolutely nothing to do with you? That he cheated because of some childhood trauma that left him feeling disconnected and detached enough to do so. That he had a change of heart in his marriage because of his own internal battles, and not because you weren't the best wife there ever was. That he "checked out" or chose an addiction over you because of unresolved, undealt-with trauma that was deep enough to pull him under a current too strong for him to swim through. Very often, the mistakes other people make that hurt us have absolutely nothing to do with us, however personal and pointed they feel. Try to see his actions through a different lens: your ex is a whole person with complex issues, not just a careless asshole who hurt your heart, hard as it may be to see it like that now. Making that kind of effort will help you heal.

Heal It

Once you're able to own your anger, release it, and take yourself out of the equation as the primary target of your ex's actions, you're on your way toward healing. Healing is everything necessary in the moving-on process, and unless you heal and let go of the hate, you won't be able to move forward.

Heal through therapy—my favorite form of working through my emotions.

Heal through self-care—remember how deserving you are of love by loving yourself first.

Heal by surrounding yourself with positivity—good friends and good energy can turn any frown upside down.

Heal by being committed to keeping the Debbie Downers, Flockers, and men who aren't worth your time out of your life.

Heal by accepting that being alone is far superior to being in bad company.

LONG STORY SHORT

✦ Your feelings of hate are a normal part of grieving a painful end to a relationship. Letting that hate fester will only serve to hurt you more and have a trickle-down effect on your children and the rest of your life, whether you intend it to or not.

✦ Before you can move forward, you have to let the hate go.

✦ Own it, exorcise it, depersonalize it, and heal it.

JOURNAL PROMPT

Write that letter to your ex, but don't send it. Just get it all out on paper.

CHAPTER 14

This Isn't About You, It's About Them

I was working with a woman who was so damn excited to leave her marriage, she gave her ex-husband just about everything he asked for. She didn't bat an eye when it came to agreeing to a 50/50 time-sharing split, didn't ask for alimony, bought him out of the house, and kept him as the beneficiary to her life insurance policy. It was a slam dunk for this guy, but sadly, a major fail for the woman, who was convinced that giving him everything meant they'd have a much easier time co-parenting their two young children. "I'm doing it for my kids," she'd argue when anyone asked why she was being so generous with the person she was divorcing. "The better I am to him, the better he'll be to them." I can totally see why she'd think that. Sadly, though, she was wrong. So damn wrong. The wrongest of wrong. His anger was not minimized by her generosity. Her good intentions did not eliminate his pain. His ego somehow ended up more bruised than before, and he treated her horribly in front of the kids and refused to be civil for any reason whatsoever.

You see, in many cases, one parent inevitably moves on faster, releases the anger and resentment of divorce a bit more easily, and tries really hard to do all the right co-parenting things. Meanwhile, the other has a hard time letting go of the past, re-hashing all of the bullshit they had to trudge through, eager to freshly ruffle feathers. No matter how good, kind, fair, and/or amicable you are, your ex may not behave as well as you—in fact, many women I speak to will say that co-parenting with a high-conflict ex sometimes feels far more challenging than being married to him.

I've said it before, and I'll say it again: you have to love your children more than you hate your ex. That being said (or shouted from the rooftops, preferably), you'll *never* find me in-sisting that you must be best friends with your ex in order to co-parent well. You don't need to have a made-for-Instagram relationship in order to do what's best for your child. But you can't hate your ex either, because, well, the porridge that's too cold doesn't get touched, and the porridge that's too hot burns. Good co-parenting means finding a Goldilocks-esque balance, somewhere between love and hate, in the land of tolerance and connection.

That means realizing that every little inch of co-parenting has absolutely nothing to do with you, or what you think is right, or sticking to your principles out of a mistaken sense of payback. It's all about them: the kids who wanted no part of this new reality.

Speaking of the principle of things, this is where I really find divorced people getting stuck as they try to forge ahead as co-parents. I hear things such as, "No, I don't think he'd be a bad father and he should technically get 50/50 time-sharing rights, but he was such an asshole! He can't always get what he wants! It's the *principle*, for god's sake." No, no. There's no room for that kind of principle in co-parenting. Relying on your sense of principle means you, yourself, are deciding what's right in a situation based on a mistake someone else made—not on what really matters most for the child.

This was a lesson I had to learn too. Trust me.

DIVORCEES AT DISNEY WORLD

When you think of Disney World, the "happiest place on Earth," I bet you don't envision recently divorced couples frolicking down Main Street USA with their four-year-old daughter. When you think of spending time with your ex-husband, I bet you don't envision a four-hour road trip in the same car together with a toddler in the backseat. Neither do I, *but that doesn't mean I didn't do it.*

Shortly after Bella turned four, she was really starting to piece together the fact that her father and I had a history once but were no longer together. She started asking lots of questions about whether or not we ever had a wedding, what my dress looked like, and why I was now going to marry someone else. For the first time in her little life, she was making observations about the fact that many of her friends had two parents that lived together in the same house, but she did not. It was clear it was beginning to weigh on her. It was even more obvious that it was high time for her dad and me to find common ground and show Bella that regardless of our living situation or marital status or general differences, she was our first priority—always would be—no matter what. It was the one thing we always agreed on.

Just eighteen months after my divorce was final, and about three months after getting engaged to my second husband, my ex and I set off on a "family" vacation to Disney World with Bella. Now, you have to understand that I didn't just wake up one day and decide to randomly take a trip with him. This trip essentially put itself together, and I'll always be grateful for how things played out. Growing up in Florida, your first trip to Disney is a sort of rite of passage. Most of my friends' children had already been there three or four times, yet neither her dad nor I had pulled the trigger. Why? Because we couldn't agree on who would take her first. Neither one of us wanted to miss the moment she first laid eyes on Cinderella's castle, or when she got to meet Elsa and Anna in real life. So, we just put the whole thing off until it just wasn't a possibility anymore.

"Mommy, all my friends have been to Disney World except me—it's not fair!" Bella shouted at me as I picked her up from school one afternoon. "Brianna said you can meet the *real* Anna and Elsa at their *real* house and take a picture with them."

Shit, I thought. *The time has finally come.*

I had been offered free tickets to the park from the Disney marketing team in exchange for some social media promotion. I hadn't yet taken advantage of this sweet perk out of fear for how Bella's father would take the news. I knew he'd be pissed that we were doing this without him, and I knew we'd have to come to a reasonable solution—fast.

"Why not take her together?" my now-husband suggested.

"Huh? Did you just suggest I go to Disney World with my ex-husband?"

"Yes, honey. You can do this—it's not about you or him. It's about a big first for Bella and giving her the opportunity to be together as a family. She's never seen you guys do that before."

God, he's good, I thought. And he was right. Bella had no recollection of her father and me ever being together, and it was time she see us do so on her behalf. I paced my room overthinking what I was about to do next, but nonetheless, took a deep breath and texted her dad asking if he'd like to join us, fully expecting him to turn me down. I knew it wouldn't be his first preference to spend time with me just as it wasn't mine. But sometimes, when you give them the opportunity, people surprise you.

"Yeah, I guess I'll get my own hotel room, LOL," he responded.

My jaw dropped. My mind raced just thinking of all the awkwardness that lay ahead. But at the same time, I knew the universe was putting this opportunity in my path as if to say, *Do this, Michelle. Awkward or not for you, Bella deserves it.*

So we did. We did the thing we both would have once deemed impossible. We took our toddler daughter to Disney World just months after finalizing our divorce. So, with our pride in our back pockets and Disney magic bands on our wrists, my ex-husband, my four-year-old, and I hopped in the car—the same car—for the long haul up to Orlando. My sweet daughter, so fixated on the fact that her parents were both in the car with her, never even bothered to question us about our destination—clearly, us being together was enough to satisfy her soul.

Our trip started out as uncomfortable and frantic as you can imagine. Being together was no longer our norm, and this awkward sense of sharing a physical space was peppered with all the tension—ALL of it. We tried our hardest to keep a friendly rapport going for the sake of that unknowing little lady sitting behind us. This situation somehow made a four-hour haul up to Orlando feel like a cross-country expedition, but, eventually, the *Welcome to Disney World* sign finally appeared in the distance. Bella's giddiness was as adorable and dramatic as we anticipated it would be.

"Oh my god, it's Mickey's house!" she shrieked from the backseat.

I knew in that instant that as difficult as these next few days might be for her dad and me personally, they'd absolutely be worth it for her.

Did the trip go swimmingly? Nope. There were plenty of moments I wanted to leave him behind at a bathroom stop and head to the next park without him. Was it easy? How could it have been? My ex, never a fan of my overly organized and slightly controlling way of doing things, was back on my schedule of departure times and Fast-Pass windows—probably a great reminder for him about how much easier his life was without me now. Was it worth all the awkward, uncomfortable tension just so that we could both experience our only child's first trip to the happiest place on Earth? Absofuckinglutely.

I realize that the idea of a trip with your ex might seem impossible to most. Hell, it seemed impossible to *me*. So don't, for one second, think that I'm pushing you to throw open your laptop and book one. I'm not. I'm suggesting that whether it's your child's next sporting event, a play at school, or a lingering conversation at the park, try finding a way to connect, in your child's best interest. You'll never regret making that effort.

NO CAMPFIRE SING-ALONGS

Struggling to find a way to connect on any level with your co-parent? Don't stress. It's not easy to find a comfortable stride in such an uncomfortable situation. Those co-parents you hear of that are having family dinners together once a week and posing for the same family Christmas photo year after year did not come out of the gate eager to hold hands and sing "Kumbaya" together. These things take time, lots of it, and, unfortunately, some trial and error. But you do have common ground: your children. And at one point, you both had at least some of your ideals aligned for what you wanted your kids' lives to look like. There are ways to come back to center on those things, no campfire sing-alongs required.

Start by making a shared list of goals/values/ideals that are equally important to both of you, no matter how different your parenting styles. Then commit to coming together on those issues the best that you can, even if it means having a simple conversation on how to handle a new bump in your child's road. For example, as different as we are, my ex and I stand on common ground when it relates to the fact that we want our daughter to:

+ Excel in school

+ Be kind and follow the "golden rule"

+ Have close relationships to her family and extended family

+ Stay committed to a sport or hobby she enjoys

+ Learn and cultivate respect for her religion

While our individual practices around homework or studying or getting together with family might look different, we both find those basic things important and are already on the same wavelength once these issues come up. If Bella has a problem at school, we're on the phone with each other within seconds, trying to work through it together. If a family event arises for either of us on one of the other's time-sharing days, we are flexible with our schedules so that she can be part of that event.

If all this sounds like a tall order, be patient and stay focused on what is important. Sometimes you just need to let the dust settle after the storm of your divorce before you can be reminded of the places where your bond with your ex was strong, so that your child can feel that, as different as Mommy and Daddy might be, they both care about what's best for me.

It just takes time, and a strong sense of knowing that you can and should love your child so much more than you hate your ex.

LONG STORY SHORT

+ You need to remember to keep your child the focus of your co-parenting relationship, not the pain or anger you harbor toward your ex.

+ You don't need to be best friends with an ex in order to co-parent well, you just need to find common ground.

+ Focus on the things that are important to both of you and vow to come together on those issues as they arise.

+ Give yourself time. This kind of thing doesn't happen overnight.

JOURNAL PROMPT

List at least three ways you and your ex can come together on common ground.

CHAPTER 15

"Mommy, What Does Ra-vorced Mean?": The Uncomfortable Questions Your Kids Will Ask and How to Answer Them

K ids say the darnedest things, don't they? In most cases, these things are funny—like when my daughter announced in the middle of the Target checkout line that her mommy likes to eat "Reese's penis." Or when she told the lady behind the checkout counter at the supermarket, who couldn't have been much older than me, that she was a "very nice old lady."

Kids. Gotta love 'em for embarrassing us whenever possible.

But if you're the parent of a child who's processing the divorce of his or her parents, sometimes it's the things they're asking that are the hardest. I've experienced these questions from my own child for years now, and I also work with clients who are struggling to find the right words to say when their children, out of nowhere, go from asking for more Peppa Pig and Pirate's Booty to casually investigating the most painful parts of your present.

As parents, it's only natural to want to shield our children from the ugly, hard-to-describe parts of life. We want to protect them from things that cause pain, and keep them young and innocent for as long as we can. Unfortunately, you'll find that you can't brush certain truths under the rug and leave them there forever, and that ultimately, your kids will need to be exposed to some harsher-than-normal realities in order to help them understand that love between adults isn't always eternal, but that your love for them is.

And that's totally okay. The truth, in the case of helping your children process their questions about divorce, will not only set you free, it will help lessen their anxiety of not quite understanding why Mommy and Daddy are in two separate homes. Truth brings clarity, and while it may hurt them to hear at first, they'll be much better off hearing certain things from their parents instead of the cruel kids on the playground.

Here's my own experience with a difficult, divorce-related question from Bella:

Sometime after she had turned four, Bella and I were on our way to preschool drop-off—a ten-minute ride that was typically rife with questions—when she asked me the one I was least prepared for: "Mommy, what does ra-vorced mean?"

I panicked. I wanted so badly for her to be distracted by a puppy being walked alongside our car or the fact that her favorite song was coming to an end. No dice. She was obviously up to speed on the fact that her dad and I were once together and now not, but it dawned on me when she asked that question that I had never actually used the term *divorce* in any of my conversations with her. She claimed to have learned the word from her friend at a playdate.

I remember slowing the car down a bit as I searched for the right words. I did a quick inventory of my brain, working hard to remember anything I had read on the topic of talking to kids about divorce. Then, I took a deep breath and answered her question: "Remember how we talked about Daddy and Mommy being married and then deciding that we'd be happier in two different homes? The grown-up word to describe that is *divorce*, and now you and your friend Rebecca have another thing in common!" I felt good about this answer. It didn't shift blame to one parent or the other, it was neutral—which I know now is very important in these conversations with our kiddos.

The truth is, Bella had asked me about my once-marriage to her father in a million different ways in the past. There was one situation in particular that I can remember as if it were yesterday, for it was as uncomfortable as it was innocent and sweet. One weekend, while cleaning out a closet in the guest room that Bella and I used as storage in our townhome, Bella came across a giant white bag hanging in the very back. "Ooh, Mommy, what's this?!" she asked, eyes wide with curiosity.

Fuck, I thought.

In that bag, the one that hadn't been opened since the morning after my wedding to her father, was my wedding gown. Crushed and rumpled in the corner of a closet I avoided digging through were the layers of hand-sewn Spanish lace I wore to become a wife for the first time. Before I could muster up an answer, Bella dove headfirst into the bag, giggling and squeaking with delight at all of the "ruffly layers." "Oh my gosh, Mommy! It looks like a princess wedding dress," she exclaimed, shocked to be in the presence of a gown so different from anything she had ever seen. Then she got quiet as she studied the dress, then studied my face, repeating this back and forth for a few moments. "Mommy, was this *your* wedding dress?" she asked with less glee in her voice, her suddenly somber tone suggesting she was uncovering a truth she hadn't expected to find.

"This *was* my wedding dress, babe. Wasn't it pretty?"

"It's sooooo pretty! Did Daddy think you looked pretty? Do you think you'll wear it again with him?" she asked innocently.

"No, baby, Mommy isn't wearing this dress again, and isn't going to marry Daddy again either. But if you love it, we can save it and maybe you can wear it one day when you're all grown up," I said to her.

"No, Mommy. I'm going to wear a purple wedding dress," she explained, as if I were some kind of idiot.

It was in that moment that I realized how little she understood of the situation between her father and me, and that I'd have to keep fielding questions like these until she was old enough to fully comprehend the facts of our divorce and what it meant for her life.

"BUT WHYYY?"

While there are endless questions your kids can ask about, well, anything, there are a few divorce-related questions that seem to pop up for many divorced parents. And while they might make you cringe or cry or a little bit of both, there *are* thoughtful, honest, and age-appropriate ways to answer these questions.

1. "You and Daddy *both* like vanilla ice cream. This means you can get back together, right?"

When I was around nine years old, my parents had a brief respite from their fighting, decided to act like co-parents, and took my brother and me to do some kind of activity together. My mind immediately wandered into how-can-I-facilitate-a-reconciliation mode. I sat down with a purple gel pen and paper and crafted two surveys with identical questions. Questions like, "What is your favorite food?" and "What is your favorite TV show?"

I was convinced that if I showed my parents that their answers were more aligned than not, I could make them get back together. You can imagine how sad I was when it didn't happen, because only my mom filled out her copy of the please-get-back-together questionnaire. That's why you need to be super clear on your answer to this question, leaving no gray area or room for interpretation. I know it feels good to give our kids hope, but it's way more damaging to give them false hope and get them excited for no reason. Finality is key here.

First, you'll want to validate their feelings. "That would make you happy if Mommy and Daddy got back together, huh?"

Next, you'll want to spit some truth. "We loved each other so much at one point, sweetie, but sometimes people change and so do their feelings. We won't be getting back together, but we will always be working together to be the best parents we can be to you."

Will there be a foot stomp followed by some tears? Maybe. Will they have unreasonable expectations for you and their daddy to reunite? Likely not.

2. "Why aren't you and Daddy married anymore?"

There are at least two certainties in life: that water is wet, and that, if you're divorced, your children will want to know why. They're going to ask it. It's inevitable. The best thing you can do before you gear up to talk to them about why you and their daddy are splitting up is know how to tell them *why*. I had a very hard time with this, so naturally I reached out to early childhood guru Evelyn Mendal, LMHC, asking how to handle this question. Here's her suggestion for a response:

> It can be so confusing to see Daddy and Mommy not married anymore, and living in separate places. Sometimes mommies and daddies decide that being married doesn't work for them and they decide to be just friends. Sometimes it may be because they fight too much when they're married, or simply because they're going to be much happier staying just friends. This is something your daddy and I decided to do, and none of it is because of anything you did—it's not your fault at all. The most important thing to know is that even if Mommy and Daddy don't love each other as husband and wife, we both love you, and will always love you just the same. We will *always* be your parents. If, at another time, you have any more questions or feelings to share, I will always be happy to listen and explain the best I can.

Will they ask again as they grow older and have a better understanding of how relationships work? Yes. Should your explanation stay consistent? Also, yes.

It may seem to us, as we see our children mature and grow, that they're ready to handle the uncomfortable details. But in reality, those can be hard to hear for even the most emotionally mature adults. Keep it clean, keep it neutral, and keep the focus on how much you *both* love your kiddos.

3. "Daddy has a new girlfriend. Will he still love me?"

This is a tough question. Not only is it a tough pill for you to swallow that your ex is with someone new, you still have to put on a brave face and answer this without bursting into tears. So before you answer it, take as many deep breaths as you need to gain composure.

Then say something like, "Yes, sweetheart, you will always be number one in your father's life! Just like Daddy and Mommy once loved each other, it's important that we find people we love to spend time with. If you ever want some alone time with Daddy, don't be afraid to ask for it, okay?"

4. "How come Daddy said that you aren't a nice mommy?"

Because he's an asshole, that's why. (Kidding. Kidding. Please don't say that.)

When I work with clients at the earlier stages of divorce and co-parenting who have high-conflict exes, we almost always run into an issue like this. Breaking the first rule of co-parenting happens to even the most well-intentioned parents, but if we give in to that temptation, our kids will internalize it. It goes without saying that talking badly about the other parent to the children is bad co-parenting business and downright damaging, but that doesn't mean it won't happen. The larger issue here is parental alienation, which, as we discussed earlier, is a term used to describe when one parent engages in behavior to distance the children from the other parent—whether through brainwashing them with misinformation about the other parent, making negative comments, or programming them to change how they feel about that parent. The term *parental alienation* has become controversial in recent years, mostly because some mental health professionals feel it should be diagnosed as a psychiatric syndrome rather than just a behavior. Either way, it's a reality for many children.

If your ex is bad-mouthing you to the children and they come looking for answers, don't freak out just yet. This unfortunate occurrence actually gives you an opportunity to have an open and honest conversation with them about something that is understandably confusing. Imagine if you *didn't* know this was happening—you wouldn't have the chance to correct it! Now, there are three types of responses you can give here: weak, retaliatory, or protective. You'll want to stick with the third option, even though it takes a little more thought. It's the one that won't add fuel to the fire. Here's what I mean:

Weak response: "Oh, he's so silly. Of course I'm a nice mom!"

Retaliatory response: "Well, your dad has no brain, and that's why he says ridiculous things."

Protective response: First, validate how they're feeling based on what they heard: "I can completely understand why Daddy saying that made you feel mad/sad/confused." Next, avoid letting your emotions get in the way and respond calmly to correct the misinformation, without letting the hot lava burning up inside you start to spew: "Mommy is always trying her best to be a good mommy. Mommy loves you more than anything." Finally, be prepared for your child to want to side with you by saying something like, "Yeah, you *are* a nice mommy. He's a bad guy for saying that!" Do not take this opportunity to sink to your ex's level and throw in a retaliatory response. Keep it protective all the way through: "Everyone is entitled to their own opinion, sweetie; like that time you loved the new Lego movie but your brother didn't. Everyone is dif-

ferent. It's what you feel in your heart about Mommy that matters."

Kids are kids. They're going to ask, pry, question, and utter
the word *why* so many times in their short childhoods; it would
be strange if they *didn't* question your marital status at some
point. Regardless of when it comes up and how it makes you
feel, remember that they deserve some truth, some validation,
and a whole lotta compassion.

LONG STORY SHORT

+ So long as the sun rises in the east and sets in the west,
kids will inevitably ask uncomfortable questions about
your divorce.

+ They deserve honesty: not false hope, no gray area—
just straight-up age-appropriate honesty.

+ Any attempts made by your ex to bad-mouth you to the
children should be met with a protective response, not a
retaliatory one. Two wrongs don't make a right.

JOURNAL PROMPT

Think of some questions you might hear from your children and
prepare a few protective responses that they can understand.
Having a plan is key.

CHAPTER 16

Getting Over Betrayal and Gaslighting, and Learning to Trust Your Gut Again

I 've always admired the women who can make a decision and just run with it, no questions asked. The ones who can point to what they want on a menu after perusing it only once. The ones who know when it's time to make a career change, letting nothing stand in their way. The ones who know automatically when they're being lied to, manipulated, or gaslit—and hit the road out of that relationship in thirty seconds or less. And while I would have killed for this type of sharp-shooting, take-no-prisoners sense of gut-led decision-making, the many times I let myself be betrayed, or questioned my own instincts, had done a number on my self-esteem. I often wondered if I could trust myself again, let alone anyone else, after years of letting other people try to rewrite the story in my head.

Can I tell you which of all the less-than-enjoyable situations I've found myself in throughout the years has had the most profound impact on my confidence and self-worth? The ones that had me questioning my own perception of reality at the hands of someone else's gaslighting techniques. It was terrifying. Like sinking to the bottom of a lake when you knew damn well how to swim, but the person you loved kept holding your hands behind your back.

Gaslighting, which you likely have experienced without realizing it, is a term that refers to what happens when someone tries to rewrite or undermine your understanding, memories, or perception of a situation. Like the woman who finds her husband texting another woman day after day, only to have him tell her when she accuses him of infidelity that she's crazy, and that the woman he's texting is "just a coworker." Like the woman who feels disrespected at every turn, and when she asks—no, begs—her partner to treat her with more respect, he makes her feel needy and annoying for wanting what she deserves. This has happened to me many times in past relationships, and despite the deep knowing in my gut that something wasn't right, I kept finding myself in relationships with a partner who dismissed my feelings. Even worse, the person doing the gaslighting would accuse me of doing the very things I felt *him* to be doing—leaving me to wonder if I really *was* crazy or just plain stupid.

By the time I got married for the first time, I had been in a series of relationships like this, which made it really hard for me to trust my gut. *Is he lying to me or am I losing it?* I'd often wonder, completely unable to distinguish between reality and bullshit.

"Why are you always looking for a fight?" I've heard in many, many of my relationships. "Why are you always making things up?" I'd be asked anytime I tried to question something fishy, like late-night texts to another woman. "Those are just your daddy issues talking," one ex-boyfriend told me many times. "You're probably accusing me of lying because you're the one hiding something." I left each of these relationships when I eventually uncovered the truth: that he was, in fact, sleeping with a girl he worked with. The truth about another ex-boyfriend's drug habit that ultimately made its way to the surface, after two years of being told that I needed mental help for thinking there was anything wrong. *What's wrong with my gut?* I always wondered. *Why can't I trust it enough to listen to it instead of begging someone else to confirm what I already know?*

I now have clients who ask me the same thing. "I was betrayed and lied to for years, Michelle; how will I ever know when my intuition is on point again?"

I'm so happy to share that it's not impossible to regain this trust in yourself, which is the only way you'll truly be able to trust others down the road. But until you turn inward and do the work that needs to be done, you'll find yourself in the same situation over and over again.

"YOU WILL NEVER FOLLOW YOUR OWN INNER VOICE UNTIL YOU CLEAR UP THE DOUBTS IN YOUR MIND."[1]

I read this quote a few years back, once I was ready for a different kind of relationship and when I felt ready to trust my gut instinct again. A study I stumbled upon during this time said something I found interesting for two reasons: it made a hell of a lot of sense, and I couldn't believe I had never thought of it before. *Anxiety and being unable to trust your gut can often go hand-in-hand.* Whoa. Talk about clarity.

So, my quest to believe in what I sensed deep down inside again started with getting a handle on my anxiety so that it could no longer suppress my intuitive decision-making, or rather, so

I could hear it more clearly among the naysayers. Therapy and anxiety medication took me really far. By the time I started dating my now-husband after my divorce, I felt so clear on my gut instincts that my confidence was soaring in a way that screamed, "No matter the situation you may find yourself in, you're okay, because you'll always know what to do."

I felt unshakable.

For some people, however, the problem isn't rooted in anxiety. It may just be a result of that one big betrayal that rocked your world, or lots of little white lies that added up to the implosion of your marriage—and there's no medication for that. But you *can* learn to trust your gut again. I've seen it happen. Here are a few concrete steps you can take on your journey of believing yourself first and trusting in your instincts to not lead you astray:

If you want to hear yourself, get quiet.

"I can barely hear myself think" is the phrase that comes to mind here. When it feels as if your life is on autopilot and you find yourself going a mile a minute in all directions, it's naturally going to be very hard to "hear" yourself. Stress clouds our judgment and undermines our confidence in our decision-making process. If you want to truly dig into your subconscious to know where it stands on a certain issue you're presented with, get quiet. Lie down. Go for a walk. Take a long, hot shower. Do whatever it is you do when you need to block out the noise of life and listen to where your mind goes. Make this a habit. Over time, you'll be able to drown out the excess noise, block out anyone trying to gaslight you or manipulate your perception, and truly hear *yourself*.

Make a list.

Make a list of all the times you let someone talk you out of believing in your gut instincts. It may feel uncomfortable to walk this path again, but getting clear on how you've been mistreated—and the times you let it happen despite knowing something was off—is important to help you harness your ability to trust and listen to yourself down the road. Prove to yourself with this list that you were, in fact, in the right, so that next time you're in a similar situation, you can listen to yourself first before anyone else.

Commit to asking yourself for advice.

You really want to call that guy you had a great first date with. Everything in your body is telling you it's the right thing to do, but alas, you text a friend—in all caps—and ask her what she would do. "Ugh, I would NEVER call first," she says, taking the wind out of your sails and making you second-guess yourself.

Because you know you can trust your instincts, you decide not to listen. Three years later, he's your husband. Do you see where I'm going with this? Stop asking people for directions to places they've never been. Ask yourself, first, so that you can take the credit for your decision-making, thus reinforcing the strength of your own knowing. Literally ask yourself, "Should I follow through on calling that guy?"

Pause, don't pounce.

Getting comfortable with trusting your gut again doesn't happen just after you've made one or two good decisions. It takes time and practice, and the ability to pause your mind and emotions for a minute or two. You want to get to a place where your emotions have fully left the building, and you can ask yourself,

Am I using my triggered/aroused/angered mind here, or am I using my gut, my deep sense of knowing, to come to this decision or understanding? There's a very big difference. A gut decision will come once you've taken the necessary time to let the flames of your immediate emotions die down.

Remind yourself that not everyone is out to manipulate you.

This can be hard to believe if someone you loved and trusted blindly has pulled one over on you, but it's true. I grew up wondering how in the world my mother could trust someone else after the level of betrayal she endured from my father. "Not all men are out to hurt and lie to women," she'd remind me. With time, with learning to trust my gut and run at the first sign of "shady," my mom's assessment proved to be right—and boy, am I happy to report it!

Accept that if it smells like shit and looks like shit, it probably is shit.

If he's hiding his phone when you come over, if money is disappearing from your joint account without an explanation, or if he turns every conversation around on you to make you look like the problem in your relationship, I have news for you: it's shit. You can throw all the potpourri you want at this big, hot pile of yuck, or you can take it for what it is and live by the Maya Angelou mantra: "When someone shows you who you are, believe them."

Once you feel you've put the work into getting back in touch with your intuition and sense of knowing, it's important that you avoid situations that make you question your gut. Or at the very least, make a promise to yourself to run the other way when your confidence in your gut intuition is challenged by someone who may be desperate for you to stay blind to the truth.

You're living your life for you now, even if you're in a new relationship. You're letting your intuition guide you, because that strong little diva inside of you always knows what's up. Rebuilding trust in yourself and others is an act of courage and takes a lot of strength but will ultimately lead you toward the right kind of relationships—the ones that would never make you question yourself. You deserve that, you really do.

LONG STORY SHORT

+ Betrayal and gaslighting can make us question our own sense of knowing.

+ Taking the steps to listen to yourself first is a critical relationship skill.

+ Build confidence in your own intuition by hearing your thoughts more clearly from a less emotional state.

+ Grab your purse and head for the door the next time someone calls you crazy for questioning what you know to be true.

JOURNAL PROMPT

When was the last time your gut sent you a message that you followed? Describe what it felt like to just "know" and how you acted upon that knowing.

Breaking Old Patterns and Understanding Your Attachment Style

Now that I've let you in on the little secret of my past relationships—that I tied myself down repeatedly to men who deceived me and made me challenge my sense of knowing—it's time we talk about breaking old patterns. Those toxic, self-worth-destroying patterns that allowed you to be gaslit and lied to time and time again. Patterns—or relationship routines, rather—may feel comforting in one sense, but I hate to break it to ya: they're killing your chances of living a really good. Fucking. Life. So is not understanding your attachment style in relationships, but I'll get back to that in a bit. Fair warning: taking this kind of look into yourself, into the patterns you've repeated that have caused your heartbreak, is not at all easy. It's the kind of work that will turn you inside out, but for good reason. Trust me, I know that you don't *really* want to wake up one day, take a good look in the mirror, and acknowledge that you, yourself, are the reason for your unhappiness. That there's no one left to blame but yourself. That all the pain could have been avoided if you'd just made better decisions. It's a rude awakening for sure, and boy was it high time for me to have one of those after my divorce. Perhaps it's time for you too.

IDENTIFYING YOUR PATTERNS

Now, I'm not saying the person you're divorcing is "bad." That person could be a wonderfully fantastic human being who does great things. What I'm saying is that it's someone who has likely been bad for *you*. Those are two totally different things—you follow? It's entirely possible you've unwittingly been repeating toxic patterns. For instance, I once let myself get attached to a really nice personal trainer after being cheated on by the guy before him. Was he a bad guy? Absolutely not. Was he bad for me? *Hell* yes. I had barely taken a moment to catch my breath after the last train wreck of a deceitful relationship before settling down with this trainer, trying to ignore the fact that he spent his days exercising with and sculpting the bodies of some really hot women.

I used to swear that I didn't have a type. I wasn't just looking for the jockish, athletic guy. My revolving door of exes didn't all fit the same "tall, dark, and handsome" profile. Some were short, light, and rugged. If I couldn't discern a pattern with the guys I was choosing, what kept happening couldn't have been my fault, right?

Wrong.

The differences I focused on were all superficial. Inside, they were all toxically similar. Something kept drawing me to them, time and time again.

I came to understand that I was my own worst enemy in relationships, especially in my marriage. Even when I began to recognize the patterns, the kinds of behaviors that were bad for me, I didn't take the time to ask the important questions. I let myself attach to people that I knew wouldn't be good for me, just to avoid being alone. I didn't ever allow a relationship to progress slowly. I took it from zero to 60 in under three seconds. I never stopped to ask myself a few important questions that could have saved me a year or two of toxicity and fighting—like, am I truly ready to date someone whose job it is to hang around hot, fit girls in sports bras all day?

YOU CAN'T THROW GLITTER ON A PILE OF SHIT AND CALL IT A MASTERPIECE

You have to stop putting yourself in situations that you know aren't right for you. The ones that leave you with questions and a stomach full of butterflies—the kind that flutter with anxiety instead of happiness. Had I not taken the time to learn how to do this, or at the very least acknowledged why I was getting myself into these situations (yes, you guessed it: daddy issues), I would not have been able to change. You have to stop setting yourself up for failure and then putting the blame on other people, because you will get absolutely nowhere in life, love, or anything else.

But before you can do this, you need to understand where the pattern first started. While I've found therapy to be the most helpful thing in uncovering the "why" behind the unhealthy attachments of my past, it's not always necessary. If you do some deep thinking and ask yourself a few uncomfortable questions, you may very well be able to get to the root of your relationship patterns so that you can make a conscious effort to break them. But it does require being completely honest with yourself, which isn't easy. Whether you can link together the patterns of your past or are just really committed to not making the same mistake twice, it's important to come to this realization now.

Here are some questions I've asked myself at different times—questions that might work to help you identify your negative relationship patterns too:

1. Is there something I struggled with in my childhood that I haven't healed yet?

For me, it was clearly the lack of love I received from my father that prompted me to attach myself to men just for the sake of feeling "attached." This has bled into other areas of my life, like friendships that were heavily one-sided (with me doing all the work, desperate for acceptance) and mistreatment in the workplace. Looking back, it was so damn obvious what my problem was, but without a hefty dose of self-healing, it's amazing what you can't see.

2. What is it about the people I've been with that has drawn me to them?

I'm a nurturer, fixer, and natural people pleaser. I took this to new heights when settling down with a new guy. I often went for the one that needed the most fixing, nurturing, and pleasing, while getting nothing in return. I thought, *Well, it doesn't matter if he's a heavy drinker; I can get him to change that, or just deal with it because he says he loves me.* Wrong. Thinking you can take a broken-down house and single-handedly make it a palace is a critical act of self-harm. It's really hard to change people, especially people who don't see a problem with their actions. Instead of putting lipstick on a pig, make a deal with yourself to stop going for the fixer-uppers.

3. What is it about the people I've dated that has
caused me pain?

Easy: their inability to be honest, emotionally attached,
and/or respectful of my feelings.

4. How have the majority of my relationships
ended?

When I finally found out the thing I thought all along. When
that thing finally came to light despite all their attempts to
make me feel delusional.

5. What are some commonalities I can find in each of
my relationships?

That they sucked the life out of me instead of helping to
fill my cup. That they forced me to question my worth and
sometimes my very existence. That they served to highlight
all of my wrongs instead of my rights. That there were more
tears than smiles.

Once you're able to answer these questions thoughtfully
and honestly, you're on your path to healing. By giving yourself
a guideline about what not to do in your next relationship, you
can ensure these sad, toxic patterns stay in the past, for good.

Oh wait, but those attachment styles . . .

DON'T EVER LEAVE ME,
'CUZ I'LL FIND YOU . . .

On the road toward healing my own bullshit, I stumbled across
a concept known as "attachment styles," based on attachment
theory, developed in the 1960s by John Bowlby, a British psy-

choanalyst who was attempting to understand the distress experienced by infants who had been separated from their parents.

It popped up again recently in a course I took on trauma and resilience. I found it so fascinating—and helpful—that it became a major focus of my coaching sessions with clients.

Attachment is the bond we form with our first primary caregiver after birth. For most of us it's a parent; for others, a grandparent or aunt or whoever has stepped in to raise us. Attachment theory posits that the quality of that bond ends up dictating the way we develop emotionally, and how we behave in future relationships. It affects how we find new partners, work to maintain relationships, and of course, how we end up leaving.

There are four attachment styles, and by the time you're through reading this chapter, you will have a good idea which style you have, and where you may need to work on yourself. My hope is that this information will be as life-changing for you as it was for me.

The four types as defined by *Scientific American* are:[1]

1. Secure: When people have a secure attachment style, they feel confident in their relationship and their partner. They're trusting, and they feel comfortable with having independence and letting their partner have independence within the relationship. They reach out for support when they need it and offer support when their partner is distressed.

2. Dismissive-avoidant: People who have a dismissive-avoidant relationship style tend to be more aloof and

feel uncomfortable with emotional intimacy. They'll commonly pull away from those they're close to if they feel a sense of rejection or are hurt by them.

3. Anxious-preoccupied: Those with an anxious-preoccupied attachment style will constantly be looking for validation, praise, and reassurance from their partners. They're inclined to jump into intimate relationships more quickly than their peers.

4. Fearful-avoidant: The fearful-avoidant attachment style defines a person who's a combination of avoidant and anxious and tends to give off mixed signals in relationships. One day they push you away, and the next, they're all over you. Think Mr. Big à la *Sex and the City*.

To better explain these attachment styles, I'll give a few examples of how they might have come into play as I navigated my relationship with my trainer ex-boyfriend. In each case, you'll see how the attachment style affects the way I respond to him.

Secure

"I know you work out with lots of hot girls every day, but I trust you! They're lucky to work out with you! Do your thing and I'll see you when you get home."

Dismissive-Avoidant

Scenario: Boyfriend comes home from a long day at the gym, later than usual, but probably only because clients were running late.

Me: Gives the silent treatment, says things really unconvincingly like "I'm fine," and goes to bed in the other room, letting resentment build while our critical communication skills deteriorate.

Anxious-Preoccupied

Trainer tells me on first date that he trains with hot fitness girls all day. My emotions are instantly triggered because my last boyfriend cheated on me at his place of work. I proceed to ignore this and date the trainer anyway because hell, it's better than being alone, right? I ask him a thousand times a day if he loves me, and if he's cheating on me. Then I check his phone behind his back. I pick fights just to gauge how he feels about me. When he starts to pull away, I accuse him even more. I beg him not to leave, like that girl from *Wedding Crashers* who annoyingly pleads in her sing-songy voice, "Don't ever leave me, 'cuz I'll find youuuu . . ."

Fearful-Avoidant

Him: I love you.
Me: Ew, you're so weird.
Him: Okay, 'bye.
Me: UGH, WHY DON'T YOU LOVE ME?!

Do you know which category you fall into now? Crazy how accurate this is, right? I can just imagine you reliving your entire relationship past while reading these descriptions. I did the same, because it all just made so much damn *sense.* In case you haven't figured it out by now, I used to live my life in the anxious-preoccupied attachment zone, but I'm so damn proud that I've now entered the secure attachment arena. It just feels better here.

Understanding your attachment style, and learning which patterns to break, is a major step up in the moving-on game. It can take you from wholly emotionally unsure to a comfortable level of emotionally evolved, and boost your self-confidence as you rediscover yourself outside of your marriage. And it'll make all the difference should you choose to put yourself back out there again.

LONG STORY SHORT

+ Identify the patterns that have kept you stuck in bad relationships.

+ Recognize your faults and shortcomings in past relationships.

+ Understand your attachment style: secure, dismissive, anxious, or fearful.

+ Knowing all these things will help you rewrite your future and the new relationships that lie ahead.

JOURNAL PROMPT

Go a little deeper with acknowledging your patterns. How does it feel to put this in perspective? How can you break these patterns moving forward?

CHAPTER 18

A New Mindset: The Glass Isn't Half-Empty or Half-Full— It's Refillable

R emember the lady in the coffee shop? The one who tried to express her sincerest condolences for the recent and untimely death of my marriage, only to be met with my snide, defensive quip? Yes, me too. I think about her often, to be honest, and wonder if she left the coffee shop that day scratching her head in bewilderment at my laissez-faire attitude toward my divorce. I wonder if she said to herself, *That Michelle Dempsey, sheesh, what a nut job!*

I often think about how I would handle this conversation today, given my growth in the four years since my split. I know exactly what I would say to her if we had a replay of this moment: "My glass isn't half-empty . . . and while maybe it doesn't seem all that half-full either, it sure is refillable."

Your glass, Mama, is totally refillable too—and it's time to fill that baby up.

WHETHER YOU THINK YOU CAN OR THINK YOU CAN'T, YOU'RE PROBABLY RIGHT

For years, I've been writing, posting, and talking all about mindset. The word *mindset* refers to the attitudes, beliefs, and thought patterns that form habits of mind. There's a specific mindset that many women find themselves in after divorce—the one that tricks them into believing that they "could never survive divorce." But the good news is, if you tell yourself that you're going to become the goddess of all goddamn goddesses after this split, it'll trick you into believing *that* just as easily. Your mindset, the shit you tell yourself about your given situation: that's what becomes your reality.

In this case, your given situation is your divorce, and your task is to move forward despite all the challenges it creates. That doesn't mean it's not hard to get stuck in the negative mindset trap of divorce.

Especially with people around you like my mom's friend in the coffee shop, looking to mourn the end of your marriage. Even today, years later, a random Instagram follower or acquaintance I haven't seen in years will make a comment like "Wow, it must really suck to not see your kid every day. Divorce seems awful; I'd hate to have to share my child with someone I wasn't married to anymore." This will temporarily take me back to a place of "oh, maybe I shouldn't have done that," before I realize that I did that, I'm doing it every day, and there's no turning back now.

It's a gut punch, definitely, but that's where I hit 'em with my mindset shift: "Yes, it's hard, but I'm so grateful that Bella has a dad who loves her and wants to spend time with her."

It all starts by realizing that your divorce is as much a rebirth as it is the death that people liken it to. Even in the practice of

Tarot reading, drawing the death card signifies new beginnings. This "death" is the end of a chapter in your life and, at the same time, a blank page on which to write the next part of your story. And guess what? The pen is in your hand now—you get to choose how you write it. With the right mindset, it's an opportunity for new experiences, an opportunity for growth, and, most important, an opportunity to live a life you may never have had if you'd stayed in your marriage. You just have to teach your mind to default to a mindset that reminds you that this pain is also filled with possibility, that your loss leaves a glass ready to be refilled to the top with good things. And naturally, I have some ideas about how you can go about doing that!

WELCOME IN THE NEGATIVE THOUGHTS—FOR A SECOND OR TWO

Adjusting your mindset to focus on the positive doesn't mean you'll never have negative thoughts. It means that you have the ability to talk yourself out of them. Your positive mindset allows you to occasionally wander into the deep, dark, self-limiting thoughts like "divorce has ruined my life," but then reminds you not to overstay your welcome in that yucky place because your positive mindset assures you that your life is not at all ruined, it's just different now. Allow your mind to wander where it needs to, when it needs to, but leave quickly. Give those negative thoughts the boot.

I once worked with a woman who got into the habit of meeting up with a friend after work each day to vent about their divorces as they walked in the park. On one hand, I loved the fact that she was outside, in the fresh air, connecting with someone who helped her validate her feelings. On the other,

I hated it, because she told me that she'd always return home from her walks feeling depleted and down. "What if you gals limited these vent sessions to only a fraction of the walk?" I suggested, before also suggesting that they spend the rest of the walk talking about the things in life they're happy about and looking forward to. This let the negative thoughts in briefly but kicked them right out the door when it was time for them to go.

FROM NEGATIVE TO POSITIVE

So much of the work that I've done personally has involved reframing and talking myself out of negative thoughts. I acknowledge how I feel and then ask myself how I can take those feelings from a "this" to a "that," from a negative to something that feels and sounds more positive. For example, from "I feel so lonely today," I shift that to "I have extra time alone today; how can I use that to my benefit?" From "Ugh, I so regret ever marrying this guy," to "I'm grateful to have married someone who taught me so many lessons about myself." I learned these techniques in therapy, and they've been a lifesaver. As you get more and more proficient in turning things from a negative to a positive in your mind, you realize your glass isn't only half-full or half-empty— it's whatever you need it to be. And you'll have a much easier time taking yourself from overwhelmed to empowered, from set back to looking forward, and, most important, from sad to strong.

REMIND YOURSELF OF YOUR BLESSINGS

One client I worked with at the very beginning of her divorce would always call me from the same spot in her home: her front porch. It had a picturesque, Southern kind of vibe. There was a massive oak tree behind her left shoulder, with a tire swing where you could just imagine generations of children had giggled. On one phone call, she carried the computer with her inside to get a glass of water, and I couldn't help but notice how stunning her home was, like something out of a catalog. As she went down the list of what was making her so unhappy on this day, I asked her to put the computer down and take a walk in and out of each room of her house, and then come back and tell me what she loved most about her home. I reminded her how lucky she was to have this home, even if the man she loved had left it. We talked about the tire swing and how much her boys loved hanging out under that tree on weekends. We eventually channeled this mindset shift into her redesigning her husband's old home office to become a room for her to read and write. She found the beauty in a situation that had nearly broken her. She did something positive with it.

So, you see, no matter what is or isn't in the glass, you still have the glass—and the power to fill it up however you want to. Do you feel me? There's something positive in every negative situation, whether you're ready to realize it or not. Instead of waking up each day focusing on what you no longer have, make it a point to honor what you *do* have. Write it down in your journal for moments when you need a reminder, and if you're having trouble coming up with a list of blessings, go look at a photo of your kids. That always helps me.

But I don't want to sound Pollyanna-ish. For some women, it truly does feel impossible to find a positive. When you desperately want to stop feeling sad, but can't. When the tears keep coming, no matter how hard you try to stop the flow. This is when I urge my clients, and all women who come to me with these feelings, to seek help. You'll never regret working with a professional who can lead you out of this slump—ever.

STOP THINKING OF WHAT COULD HAVE BEEN

It didn't last. It didn't turn out how you wished it would. There's no amount of "what-if-ing" you can do that will change this fact. Instead of wasting energy thinking about what could have been, focus on fixing the things in yourself that may have contributed to what happened. That way, you set yourself up for future success.

START THINKING ABOUT THE REFILL

Who said the glass has to be half-anything? Maybe in this chapter of your life, the glass overflows with love. With self-confidence. With an abundance of joy and a renewed sense of self. Maybe this is when you finally take the time to do the things that your soul aches to do. Maybe it's when you finally give in to your deepest desires. Maybe it's when you put yourself out there after doing the healing you need to do with a new outlook on relationships, allowing you to attract the healthiest kind for your heart and mind. Maybe, just maybe, this is when you learn to live your very best life.

LONG STORY SHORT

+ Your glass isn't half-empty or half-full, it's refillable.

+ You have the power to shift your mindset.

✦ Allow yourself to feel all the feelings, but don't live in the negative ones.

✦ Flip your perspective on its head and find the good in everything.

✦ Refill your glass exactly how you want to—this is your moment to rewrite your story.

JOURNAL PROMPT

Start rewriting your story. Where do you want to see yourself in a year? Five years? How will it feel?

CHAPTER 19

Sassy, Classy & a Little Bit Badassy—Your Best Self After Divorce

Around the same time that my marriage was imploding, bodysuits came back in style. Call it the luck of the draw, good timing, or sheer coincidence, but it was high time for me to put a little more effort into myself. I had been wearing plain white tee shirts and boxy work blouses for three years at this point. Since getting pregnant and having Bella, I'd resigned myself to the idea that looking sexy and desirable had no place in my life anymore, as a toddler and her Cheez-It crumbs clung to me like white on rice. But I missed dressing up, even just for myself.

So, I bought a bodysuit. It was black and laced up the front with black laces that came down to just below my cleavage. It made me feel sexy and powerful and strong. And it showed off my shoulders—which were the one part of my body that seemed to have made it through childbirth and a rocky marriage unscathed. I loved this bodysuit *and* my shoulders. The only problem was, I had nowhere to wear it.

Date nights weren't really happening anymore. Girls' nights were low key and casual, not worthy of such a form-fitting, showstopping ensemble. That's what I thought, at least, until one night, a single girlfriend asked if I wanted to meet her for drinks downtown. My ex, to whom I was still married, happened to be out of town at a bachelor party, and my mom was excited at the idea of coming over to watch Bella so I could go have some fun.

"You need a night out, Michelle," she said. "Enjoy it."

I don't know if I was more excited about the idea of getting out of the house and letting loose, or just being able to wear this damn bodysuit that sat lonely in my closet among the rows of Banana Republic silk blouses and conservative button-down tops. If I'm being honest, it was the bodysuit. Totally the bodysuit.

I threw it on with a pair of good jeans (not the ones I wore to sit on the floor at music class with Bella) and some heels. It was the most myself I had felt since before becoming a mom.

"Wow, Mish. Looking good," my mom said as I paraded into the living room with a twirl. I sent my husband a selfie. No answer. I checked my phone repeatedly to see if he'd give me so much as a thumbs-up or any form of the validation I so desperately needed from him. Still no answer; he was busy with friends, and I was busy being overly needy, as usual.

I met my friend at one of our favorite restaurants on a busy street in downtown Fort Lauderdale. It was the kind where you didn't mind waiting for a table because hanging out at the bar until your name was called was entertainment enough. I hadn't been "out on the town" in ages, and, ever since that time, I'd been living a life of not feeling all that desirable or wanted. I wasn't sure if I still "had it," which is a tough way to feel as you're watching your marriage crumble to bits.

A good-looking guy offered to buy me a drink. I wanted to say yes but knew that I shouldn't—I was married, after all. But damn, the offer felt good. "No thanks, I'm just hanging with a friend tonight," I responded with a smile. It's not that I didn't want to be hit on, just that I wasn't ready for that kind of interaction. Getting hit on felt good; really good, if I'm being completely honest. It was the exact kind of validation I needed that night— the kind that came from knowing that even if my husband never responded to the photo I sent him (or never looked at me again, for that matter), I still had it. That thing that interested other men enough to want to buy me my next gin and tonic.

Looking back, I feel silly when I think about how much that meant to me, how trivial and meaningless the twelve-second interaction with a hot guy at the bar was, but at the same time, that night was important to me for a few reasons not having to do with the bodysuit:

It reminded me of the power of a girls' night out.

It gave me a look ahead into what single life might be like.

It gave me the opportunity to feel like my best self.

WHEN IN DOUBT, WEAR THE BODYSUIT

First things first: let's talk about your self-esteem or lack thereof. I'm not going to sugarcoat it: your self-esteem will likely take a nosedive after your split, regardless of which one of you chose to end the marriage. The person you had committed yourself to, the one who has seen you at your best, worst, and most bloated, is gone. Chances are, he didn't do you any favors in the self-esteem department, either, as the last few months or years of marriage usually lack passion, intimacy, and compliments. This is normal. Wondering if you'd still be desirable to a future love interest is normal. I don't think I've met a woman yet who hasn't wondered this, without understanding the dire importance of finding *herself* desirable first. Like with the bodysuit. Had no one offered to buy me a drink the night I wore it, had my mom not complimented me, and had I just put it on from time to time around the house, it still would have given me a major confidence boost, the kind I needed as I closed the door on my marriage. I realized that there were so many other ways to get back to my most badass self, and most of them had nothing to do with the hot drink-buying guys at the bar.

When I'm helping women go from "why me" to "damn, it feels good to be moving on," there are a few things I recommend for that Stella-got-her-groove-back vibe.

Do What Feels Good

We all have sides to us that we tend to tuck away in our marriages. These are the things we felt silly doing in front of our husbands, or the things that we just didn't have time for anymore. If you were a *Sex and the City* fan back in the day, you'll remember the episode about SSB: Secret Single Behavior. For Carrie, it was eating a stack of Saltines and jelly while standing in her kitchen pants-less, reading *Vogue*. For Charlotte, it was staring at her pores for hours on end in her magnifying mirror. Odd? Maybe. But it just felt good—like a release of some kind.

For me, it was wandering the aisles of Home Goods with a girlfriend without having to justify what I spent or why I needed another decorative bookend. Getting in bed early to watch whatever the hell I wanted with a bag of kettle corn–flavored Pop-

Corners within reach. Long walks around the golf course with my headphones on and some old-school hip-hop blasting in my ears. These things made me feel alive. They were the things I never really did when I was married, for one reason or another. Doing them again made me feel good, and even the smallest acts of self-indulgence can be wildly confidence-boosting.

Move Your Body

For months I had been dying to try a boxing class at my local gym. Before my split, I hadn't allowed myself time to exercise. I had been so bogged down with stress, trying to build my business and working every waking moment that Bella was in school. My only form of exercise was taking her for walks in the stroller in the late afternoons, which helped, yes, but didn't give me the same endorphin boost I knew I was missing. The idea of a good old-fashioned sweat session called to me all the time, but when I was still married, I felt irresponsible answering. I felt guilty at the thought of leaving Bella with a sitter so I could take an hour for myself at the gym. I wanted it so badly, but didn't want to have to justify it to my husband.

Not long after settling into life as a single mama, I signed up for the boxing class everyone had been raving about, making it my first stop of the day after dropping Bella off at preschool. I didn't have to justify this decision to my ex, or to anyone else, for that matter. I was on my own time and doing what I wanted to do with it. I was nervous and a bit insecure entering the gym again, since I knew this was a place that true fitness enthusiasts frequented. I went anyway and vowed to be inspired by the strong, sexy people around me. As the music blasted, I went to town on punching the shit out of the boxing bag, which not only boosted my endorphins, it lowered my stress BIG time. I immediately purchased a package of classes and began showing up twice a week. On the days in between, I worked out alone or with a trainer to push me a bit harder. Three months into my split, I felt stronger than I had felt in years, which was a huge confidence boost that I needed so much.

Start Saying No

Think of all the times you said yes when you wanted to say no. Maybe it was to that mom who asked you to take her kids home with you after school because she had an appointment. You were already exhausted but felt bad about refusing, so you went along with it. Maybe it was to that date with the "nice guy" your mom's friend tried setting you up with after your split. You knew in advance he wasn't your type but didn't want to let anyone down. It's time to stop this nonsense. You've already said no to continuing a marriage that wasn't working out for you, and that's probably the hardest no to say, so you need to start applying this tiny-but-mighty word to the rest of your life when necessary.

A few years back, I wrote an article in which I explained why I believed the word *no* to be the sexiest in the English language. Sexy? Yes. Because of the control you immediately take when saying those two letters. The word *no* allows you to harness your power, go with your gut, and make choices that truly feel right, turning on *all* of your self-confidence receptors.

Schedule Girls' Nights

Girls' dinners. Girls' drinks. Girls' trips. Get it on the calendar and make it happen. Being with good friends, the kind that are always down to empower and uplift you, truly helps put the wind back in your sails after a divorce. I remember my mom having a crew of two other divorced girlfriends when she was going through her own, and they did everything together, from taking us kids on road trips to taking themselves out for fancy dinners in New York City. It was the girl time that filled their cups up most, and the same rang true for me.

Journal

You knew I was going to say it. I had to. Because my journal and I spent so much time together in my quest toward feeling like my best, most badass self again after divorce, I want you to do the same. I wrote about what kind of partner I envisioned for myself in the future, how I wanted to feel about myself, and what I would do to make it happen. I made promises to myself, shared secrets, and used my journal as a tool to keep looking forward instead of behind me—which kept me full of excitement and wonder, teeming with energy at the idea of new opportunities in the life that lay ahead.

Getting back in touch with your best self after a split is so damn necessary and liberating. It isn't all that hard, either, once you commit to making the effort. Even on your worst days, you'll be able to find something that makes you feel good, and hey, if all else fails: wear the damn bodysuit.

LONG STORY SHORT

✦ You deserve to feel like your best, most badass self now more than ever.

✦ Feeling confident after a divorce has nothing to do with the opposite sex.

✦ Find the things you love doing and do them often: Move your body. Call some friends. Write your heart.

✦ When in doubt, wear the bodysuit.

JOURNAL PROMPT

What makes you feel your sexiest? When was the last time you felt truly desirable and sexy?

CHAPTER 20

Dos and Don'ts of Dating
After Divorce

You've refrained from the impulses you felt early on in your split, the urge to just throw yourself at some new guy for the sake of being touched. You've worked through the deep need to have someone, anyone, stroke your ego, because it had been so damn long since anyone made you feel good. You've held back until you did the work on yourself, and I'm proud of you, because that's not an easy thing to do. You've waited until your mind was fresh and focused, your heart felt healed, and you got really clear on which mistakes you wouldn't make twice. Oh, and not to mention, you've finally realized just how much love and respect you truly deserve.

Nice work, Mama.

Now it's time. You feel ready. Not just to get under someone new, but to crawl out from beneath the rock you've been healing under and potentially meet someone for the long haul—someone to be by your side through the new life you've created for yourself. A partnership. None of that once-in-a-while late-night "WYD?" shit.

It's time for the real stuff.

THE SECOND LIFE

"Ugh, you and Spencer are sooooo cute," my friend would exclaim every time she and I went for a walk or caught up by phone. "I want that tooooooooooo," she'd whine when comparing her life to my life with my second husband.

"You're going to have it," I reassured her. "You kinda just have to leave your marriage first, LOL."

This friend of mine was unhappily married, comfortably, for a long time. She and her ex-husband both knew they were unhappy, but since there weren't any pressing, dramatic issues, or incessant fighting for that matter, she was having a hard time making the decision to move on. Until one day, she got really clear on the fact that she wanted good love. Not just the comfortable, safe kind. The kind that filled up her soul inside and out, and made her feel as if this was where she was always supposed to be.

"I feel like this can't really happen in real life—the kind of love you and Spencer have," she'd insist. "It's like a fairy tale!"

She hadn't even tried yet to meet someone who made her own life feel like a fairy tale, but I knew it was coming for her. I knew this the same way I know that any woman who has healed and gotten clear on her self-worth and put her priorities in order has that pot of gold at the end of the rainbow waiting for her if she wants it. I just *knew* it. Because if you aren't done with love yet, if you feel like a love awaits to make up for all the pain you've endured, you're bound to manifest it.

Three years later, she has just moved into a beautiful new home with her beau and her daughter, and her wedding is in the works. She's created her "second life," as I like to call it, and I love to tell her I told her so.

So how exactly does one find love again in someone else after a split? It all starts with dipping your toe in the uncomfortable world of dating. Setting yourself up on a few dating apps, allowing friends to fix you up on blind dates, being open to finally flirting back with that guy you always see at Starbucks— this is how you get back out there, scary as it seems. But as you approach this new adventure, there are a few key dos and don'ts. Here are some guidelines to help your second life take flight:

Be open to new experiences.

When Spencer asked me where I'd like to go on our first date, my knee-jerk reaction was to suggest the same restaurant my ex and I loved. It felt familiar, I missed their grilled octopus, and I hadn't been there in ages.

"How about this new restaurant/bar in downtown Miami with live music?" he suggested.

Ugh, downtown Miami, how pretentious, I thought. But I knew it was time to let go of the familiar. Why the hell should I kick off something new in the same old place I used to have heated arguments with my ex? *Yes* to downtown Miami turned into stepping out of my comfort zone and into a world far, far away from the one where I already lived.

Stop imagining that each date will lead to marriage.

Don't put that kind of pressure on yourself, because expectations like that can lead to some serious disappointment. Yes, you want your second life to begin, but not every date will be the one that kicks off the whirlwind romance you have in your head. Treat each first date as what it is and nothing more: a first date. If a second date happens, yay. If not, oh well. There will be more.

Don't waste the first date talking about your ex.

It's inevitable that the topic of your divorce—and possibly his—will come up. Keep it short, to the point, and avoid letting your emotions enter the conversation at this point: "Yes, we got divorced—not the thing people dream of—but we're co-parenting the best we can now." I've had many clients return home from a first date with their head spinning after having to endure cocktails, appetizers, and a heavy entrée of anger and resentment toward an ex being spewed from all ends by their date. Not only is this a big turnoff, it sends the message that you're not over your ex yet.

Don't let your desire to find love again cloud your judgment.

It's important to not let desire cloud your judgment, or blind you to the giant red flag waving about this guy's head as he says, "Yeah, I've cheated on all my exes, and I'm not sure if I want kids." See the flag, end it there, and keep it moving.

Be brutally honest.

Lay all your cards—every last one of them—face up on the table in clear view for your date to see. If the questions come up organically, answer them as honestly as you can. You have nothing to lose by being honest, except for a guy who doesn't deserve you and your truth. You want to get married again one day? Admit that. You want more kids or don't? Make it clear. You hate long walks on the beach but love slow strolls to the couch?

Say it. Don't be someone you're not on your quest for this second life.

Don't be shy about being a single mom.

"Who will want to date a single mom?" I've heard from friends, clients, and even my own subconscious at one point. Well, plenty of people, actually, because there are single dads out there too. Don't be ashamed at any point in your dating journey to share how much time you spend with your kids, and your commitment to putting them first. You're a mother now, and these things are perfectly normal. The right man will love and respect you more for it. Anyone who seems reticent about the fact that you have kids isn't the right person for you.

Don't force chemistry—but take full advantage of it when you find it!

Chemistry will or won't exist with the new people you're dating. It's as simple as that. If there isn't any on the first date, it's likely there won't be on the second date. Don't try to force it, or take it as a sign that you're not dateable and amazing. Sometimes two wonderful people just don't have that attraction, for whatever reason. When you *do* feel the chemistry, however, go for it. Act on it. Lean in for the kiss. See what it feels like.

When you meet a great one, be patient and take it slow.

You're older and wiser now. Plus, you have kids in tow. When you find a relationship that feels real—the kind that whispers to your heart *I'm here to stay*—slow down a bit. Invite him into your life and your kids' lives gently, drop by drop, to help things go more smoothly. Let this relationship blossom organically, like all the best ones do. Harness your patience with this new par-

amour and learn to adjust to his life—and the children he may
be co-parenting—just like he'll have to do with yours.

Speaking of kids . . .

Because I'm a mom, it was important to me that I dated someone who not only understood parenting, but the complexities of
co-parenting as well. But that's just me. I know plenty of women
who don't want to deal with someone else's children and ex-wife,
and that's okay too. Know where you stand on this issue well
before you begin dating. If you're a hard no on dating someone
with children, don't say yes to the date. If he seems amazing but
says he's not that into kids, you know what you have to do.

If anything doesn't feel right, honor that, and keep it moving.

You're back in touch with your gut now, so this should be easy. If
something smells fishy, it probably is. If things aren't adding up
in your conversations, don't try to do the math, just go. Honor
that calling from your gut that says, *Um, I'm not sure about this
one*, and cut your losses—before *you* end up emotionally cut.

Remember to leave space for you.

Finding a new love and starting your second life doesn't mean
losing yourself. The best thing you can do as you start out on
your new life in love is remember to take care of you first. Your
self-care matters, your ideas and opinions matter, and your ability to function as an independent woman in society matters—
big time. Don't live your life for the relationship; rather, let the
relationship become a special part of the new life you've created
for yourself.

Oh, and Google him.

With all this in mind, it's time to get to dating after divorce. You deserve to enjoy it, to be enjoyed inside and out for the beautiful, strong, healed woman you've become. So get it!

LONG STORY SHORT

+ If you feel healed and ready to date, go for it!

+ It all starts with dipping your toe in the sometimes uncomfortable world of dating, knowing it gets easier with each "dip."

+ Don't treat each date like your potential next husband—take the pressure off.

+ Unapologetically own who you are, your single motherhood, and all your wants and needs.

+ If it looks like a red flag and waves like a red flag, it probably is a red flag.

+ Don't force chemistry. Enjoy the chemistry when it presents itself.

+ Remember not to make the relationship your whole world, but rather, a part of the world you've created for yourself.

JOURNAL PROMPT

What are some must-have qualities in your next partner? Non-negotiables? Get clear on these now!

CHAPTER 21

Getting Laid After Divorce, Part 2

There comes a time in every woman's post-divorce journey when the itch is finally ready to be scratched. When she not only shaves above the knee for the first time in ages, she uses real shaving gel instead of bar soap to get the job done. When the beige-colored, worn-out undies get left behind for a satin thong in some dangerous red or black. When the bra matches the undies. When the pain and hurt of her divorce is beginning to feel like a distant memory, and her body aches to start making some sexy new memories with someone else.

So, she slips on "those" jeans—the ones that always make her feel her sexiest. She pays extra attention to where she sprays her perfume on this night, takes one last look at herself in the mirror, smiles at the sight of her sexy bodysuited silhouette on her way out the door, and thinks, *It's go time, baby. Let's do this.*

Whenever I speak to clients about the notion of sex after divorce, I'm reminded of a friend who treated her first sexual experience after her divorce like the second coming of Jesus. It was a *big* deal. Sasha Fierce, as we'll call her, had been a sexual being for her entire adult life. She was the friend who sat around the dinner table at girls' night in shock when her friends discussed wanting to avoid sex with their husbands. For her, sex was the best part of any relationship, so it was no wonder that once she put herself back out into the world—or back under the covers, I should say—it was bound to be a milestone moment for her.

Sasha set out on her first date a few months after reentering the single-gal arena, which was a few months after the end of her first marriage. She prepped for this date for days, as she and the lucky guy had been chatting it up for weeks—by text all day and on the phone at night. "This night is going to change every-thing," she told me, and I kind of had a feeling that she was right. Something seemed different about her being back in the dat-ing game this time around. She'd always loved sex, but now she had enough self-confidence to ignore advances from men who didn't seem worth her time, to be more selective about who she got involved with. I talked her through the whole day leading up to the big first date, giving her advice on what to wear and vali-dating her excitement. She was nervous in all the best ways, but absolutely sure about her choice to make this night a good one.

I woke up the next morning to a text that read, *It happened! I lost my post-divorce virginity. It was as hot and sexy and magical as I knew it would be.* And just like that, she got laid after divorce— on the first night of the first real date she'd let herself go on since splitting from her husband.

Now, I know what you're thinking: sex on the FIRST night of the FIRST date after divorce? Sure, it seems a little ballsy and forward, but she had always been fearless and sex-positive, and she trusted her gut. That whole "everything will change after to-night" feeling proved to be true. They're married now.*

*Results not typical.

Here's the thing I believe about sex after divorce: while you don't necessarily need to go for the gold on the very first date, I don't think you have to wait around six months for a letter jacket and a promise ring to let him get in your red satin panties, either. You're older now than the last time you dated. You're wiser, and, frankly, have way less time for bullshit. If the chemistry is good and the object of your affection seems solid (i.e., not married, not sketchy, not booking up three dates the same night as yours), why wait around to do the deed? Find out early on if those butterflies you feel each time he texts you translate into something magical in the bedroom. Sex and intimacy are important in a relationship, and, after coming out of a bad marriage—one that may well have ended up sexless as the relationship deteriorated—you deserve to have that kind of powerful, passionate connection. Why waste your precious time dating someone for months, only to find out he's an A on paper but a D-minus on your 1,800-thread-count sheets?

Everyone has their own timeline, but regardless of when you hop back in the sack with someone, I do want to share a few truths about sex after divorce—what you can expect, and how to get through each hurdle without feeling like you're making a mistake.

IT'S NORMAL TO FEEL INSECURE

As confident and ready as you might be to let someone new explore your body, the truth is, your body is different now. You've had a baby or three, you might have breastfed, and things probably aren't as tight and perky as they used to be. It's normal to feel slightly insecure about your body the first time you take it all off for your new love interest. I remember being super self-conscious about my C-section scar, but trust me: it went undiscussed for a long time. Remind yourself that whatever package you're bringing to the table these days is a powerful one. It has created new life, withstood the pain of divorce, and marched you right into an empowered new world. The man who's lucky enough to have you won't be focusing on that little belly bulge— I swear it.

IT'S NORMAL TO FEEL LIKE YOU'VE DONE SOMETHING WRONG THE FIRST TIME YOU HAVE SEX AFTER DIVORCE

"I feel like I cheated on my husband even though we haven't been together for months!" is something I've heard from both clients and friends. This isn't uncommon. After years of being committed to one person, it's going to feel a little naughty to let someone new explore your body. Try to let go of this feeling, however hard it is. You absolutely deserve to move on in the physical sense, and you deserve to enjoy it too. Remind yourself that you're no longer physically or emotionally connected to your ex, nor are you obligated to uphold any more vows that would prevent you from being with someone new. Give yourself permission to go for it.

IT MAY TAKE MORE TIME THAN USUAL TO LET GO AND ENJOY

If your trust was broken in your marriage, particularly by infidelity or abuse of any kind, it may take time for you to be able to truly let go and feel confident during sex again. This is one of the reasons why I warned against sex immediately after your split. Give yourself time. You need to let yourself travel through each stage of those yucky post-divorce emotions so that you can take back your sexual power. If you experienced sexual trauma on any level, there's no better way to help yourself heal from this than therapy, and that's an avenue well worth exploring. Be patient with yourself. It'll be worth it.

IT'S OKAY TO ASK FOR WHAT YOU WANT

Did you spend endless nights underneath your ex wishing he would try something new but feeling too embarrassed to ask? Now is your chance to have the sex you always wished you were having. Don't be shy about asking for what you want, how you want it, and when. Remember that the person you're sleeping with now is likely also harboring some feelings of insecurity. Men feel a lot of pressure around sex too. They feel pressure to perform, and perform well, and pray that their penis size doesn't completely disappoint. And if he's divorced too, he's got his own baggage. For this reason, it can feel really refreshing to have someone else—you—take the lead from time to time. If you want it, ask for it.

IT'S OKAY TO TAKE A
GOLDILOCKS APPROACH

The date may have been perfect and you may already be thinking of him as the ideal man to settle down with in your second life, but then the sex was just okay. It's perfectly okay to decide you don't want to pursue a relationship with someone based on how he does or doesn't fulfill you sexually. It's only natural that it may not be a slam dunk the first few times when both of you are nervous, so it's probably worth sticking with it for a bit if you really like him otherwise; but if this becomes a pattern for longer than a few months, assume it may not get better. Imagine how you'd feel committing to a whole new life with someone with whom sex feels dull. It's okay to test the waters—aka, try each bowl of porridge and bed until you find the combination that's juuuuust right. It worked for Goldilocks and it's important that you don't settle now, not after all you've been through.

PROTECT THYSELF

I'm sorry; forgive me for having to go to this place, but perhaps it's just the mom in me. If you're going to protect your heart, do the same for your body and wrap it up. If he respects you, he'll agree to this barrier—don't take no for an answer!

KNOW THAT POTENTIAL REJECTION IS PART OF THE PACKAGE—AND DON'T LET IT DERAIL YOU

There's no guarantee that the person you're now dating and letting yourself have sex with is going to stick around forever. No one has a crystal ball, so even if it feels like you've found someone who hits all the marks you're looking for *and* makes your time in bed feel otherworldly, he could very well decide that you're not the right person for him. Naturally, this will leave you feeling rejected—you're human, after all. You'll feel foolish for having trusted someone again with your body. You'll wish you'd never let the sex happen. You'll wonder if maybe your ex-husband was as good as it was going to get.

Let me break this down for you real quick:

1. No, you're not foolish. This is how you rediscover who you are and who is right for you after a split.

2. Yes, you *should* have let it happen. You can't get it right until you try.

3. Hell no, your ex-husband was definitely not as good as it was going to get.

If you feel rejected when a sexual experience or budding relationship goes wrong after divorce, instead of giving in to self-doubt, consider it another learning opportunity. It's very rare to get everything right on the first try like Sasha Fierce. Keep going! The right one will stick.

In conclusion, my sexual, ready-to-pounce, lovely ladies: have sex when you're ready. Have all the sex. Have the sex you have always dreamed of having. Vanilla sex. Chocolate sex. Salted caramel cayenne pepper sex. You've done the work to overcome the pain. You've successfully entered a brand-new era of your life in which you get to do the things you've dreamed of doing for so long. You're more confident and more aware now. Put on the satin panties, spray the perfume below your belly button, and get back on the saddle.

LONG STORY SHORT

✦ Sex after divorce feels best when you're truly ready for it.

✦ You don't have to wait for months and months and a promise ring to let someone new explore your body. Better you know up front whether it's going to be good or not.

✦ As much as you want sex, you may still have insecurities about your body. Own them and don't let them hold you back.

✦ You aren't cheating on your husband. He isn't your husband anymore.

✦ You deserve to have good sex.

✦ You may feel rejected, but you can always get back up and try again.

✦ Enjoy your new sexual experiences—you deserve every single one.

JOURNAL PROMPT

Write about the parts of you that you love. Why would someone else love them too?

CHAPTER 22

Will I Die Alone?

I can't believe he did this to me!" an acquaintance of mine sobbed on the phone shortly after learning of her husband's affair. "After all these years, how can he just leave me and us and our whole world as if none of it ever mattered?!"

I felt for this woman. Her husband literally upped and left her out of nowhere, after she had several miscarriages, four children, incredible business success, the deaths of both her parents, and his early-stage cancer. He threw it all away for some bottle-service waitress at a club downtown. Naturally, the woman had every reason to feel (and sound) as if she'd had the wind knocked out of her. But if I only had a dollar for every time I'm asked the question that came out of her mouth next:

"Will I die alone, Michelle? Please just tell me I won't. I *can't* die alone."

"Are you currently dying, that you know of?" I asked her.

"No," she replied, almost annoyed that I asked her the question.

"Do you have anyone in your life who loves you?" I asked again.

"Well, yeah, of course I do."

"Then you probably won't die alone," I told her, before reminding her that "alone" and "lonely" are two very different things.

As a survivor of the can't-survive-without-a-man mindset, I understand all too well the anxiety of being alone. I, too, had fears of being the old lady who lived alone with her golden retriever or multiple cats, watching reruns of *Sex and the City* with curlers in my hair and popcorn in my lap until they carted me off to the old-age home. Look: the idea of being alone for the rest of your life can be scary. I worked through those feelings and conquered them by knowing I could be happy without needing the validation of a man in my life. But it took time and effort. If you're feeling panicked about the prospect of a life without a partner, I feel you, and I truly want to help you through this— because this is the kind of fear that can blind you to all the other beauty in your life, the beauty that has nothing to do with relationships at all.

But first, let's get back to that whole alone/lonely thing. Here's what I've learned about the difference between those two concepts:

1. You can be physically alone but not feel lonely.

2. You can be married and have a house full of kids but feel incredibly lonely.

Confused? Let me break it down:

I'm sitting alone in my office right now, writing this chapter. But I'm not lonely, because I'm doing the thing I love. And frankly, I'm happy there's no one interrupting me and asking me for a snack, an opinion, or where his keys are. Alone means sitting in solitude, a situation that can change if I just stand up, walk out of this room, put on some shoes, and visit a friend or go to the mall.

Lonely, though—that's something else. Loneliness is much more of a feeling than a physical state; a sense of longing, a belief that something is missing. The word *lonely* itself makes my heart hurt, thinking of the older woman who lives in my grandma's neighborhood who sits at her window day in and day out, as if she is searching for something. As if she never found a way to fill the gaping hole in her heart that was left behind by something that left her life. *Loneliness*, not *solitude*, is what this scorned woman on the other end of the phone line was truly scared of, and when we're knee deep in pain, transition, and confusion, that feeling is bound to be heightened. Lonely is how I remember feeling in my first marriage, as so many women will say they felt when they were committed to the wrong person. Often, ironically, it's less lonely to be single than to be in a marriage that's not serving you, that you know must eventually end.

IT'S ALL UP TO YOU

Because I'm so frequently asked the question about dying alone, I've had a lot of practice doling out advice and suggestions. I've also had the pleasure of sitting back and watching all the same women go on to become their truest and happiest selves after divorce, laughing when they ask, "Oh my god, do you remember how scared I was to be alone?" Because that's exactly the thing: if you stay stuck in your fear, you will absolutely feel lonely. You won't be able to find the beauty in having a Saturday night to yourself. You won't be able to turn down a date that you're hardly interested in, because you're so scared you'd be passing up a chance of having somebody—anybody—pay attention to you. You won't be able to take your life as it is now and make something really fucking great of it, regardless of whether or not you share your bed with someone else. If you work through this fear and realize that alone isn't so bad, you're already halfway home.

I once worked with a woman who was so unsure of what to do with her alone time, so scared to be left at home with nothing but just her thoughts, that she would go out drinking with friends to pass the time. She'd start drinking at home by herself and then send out a text to friends to see who was at the neighborhood bar, go there and drink until last call, make it home, and wake up past noon the next day, completely forgetting what went on the night before. Then she'd spend the rest of the day feeling shitty: crying, questioning her worth, wishing for more, rinse and repeat.

During a Friday afternoon session, she expressed her fear about having nothing to do that upcoming Sunday. She mentioned trying to find plans. I told her not to. I told her that I wanted her to avoid the impulse of doing something, anything, just to avoid what it felt like for her to be alone.

"Michelle, I *can't*. Are you kidding? I'll die!"

"You will not die," I told her. "You will survive the day, and feel empowered for having done so."

"No, literally, Michelle. I'll go crazy. I don't have my kids. I won't know what to do with myself."

So, we made her a schedule.

I asked her to avoid drinking the night before so that she could wake up with a clear head. Then I suggested she go for a long walk in her neighborhood. Then make herself a yummy breakfast. Then plop down on the couch and read a book. Then reorganize a closet that needed some attention. Then maybe make a sandwich. Then do her food shopping and meal prep for the week. Then call a friend she had been meaning to catch up with. Then spend a solid hour with her journal (as you've probably noticed, none of my clients get out of jail journal-free). Then cook herself a big, decadent dinner from the recipe she had saved on her phone. Then, I instructed her to write down how all of it felt, and to bring that to our next call.

"Holy shit, Michelle, it was hard, but I made it," she told me, sounding accomplished and proud.

"I love to say I told you so!" I shrieked, also feeling accomplished and proud.

From that day on, she agreed to make herself a list of things to do each time she was feeling anxious about time alone. She tinkered around the house, redesigned an entire room, bought every book I suggested, became a self-help junkie, and even enrolled in an online educational program she had long been interested in.

"It's easier being alone now," she said to me. "It doesn't feel so lonely anymore."

All it took was refocusing herself away from her fear—and it was worth all the effort. Here are a few things you can do to shift your perspective so that the concept of being alone can feel less scary, and help you understand that loneliness is a state of mind you can change:

Be your own best friend.

Learn to love your own company. Listen to yourself the way you would a best friend. Honor her thoughts, wants, and needs. Make it a point to carve out time to hang out with your "best friend" and look forward to it the same way you would a physical meeting with friends. Put your friendship with yourself first, and you'll find enough fulfillment in that relationship to make it hard to feel lonely.

Stop comparing yourself to others.

It's not hard to sit alone in your bed after a divorce, looking at social media photos of your friends with their husbands and kids, and think that your life sucks because they have *that* and you don't. You know very well that a photo doesn't tell a whole story, that even the happiest of married couples have their own shit to deal with, and that those kids had to be bribed with lollipops and a fear of Mom's wrath to stand and smile for a photo. The point is this: the grass isn't greener somewhere else, it's greener where you water it. If you're constantly comparing yourself to others, to what they have or don't have, you'll always feel a sense of longing. That's a trap you can totally avoid sinking into by simply remembering that "comparison is the thief of joy," as Teddy Roosevelt wisely said.

Find an outlet.

My grandma, whom we refer to as Nanny, lost her husband, my beloved grandpa, in the summer of 2020. They had been married for just shy of sixty-seven years. Because we were so close, my main focus became making sure she didn't feel lonely. In the days and weeks after his death, I'd call her three times a day to make sure she was keeping busy, to remind her to have some lunch, to ask if she was okay. My grandma and I have always had a relationship like this, but I was taking it to an extreme because I was just so damn worried about how her emotional state would shift after being alone for the first time in seventy years. Finally, one day, after I called to ask her the same questions again and make small talk, she shouted at me, "Why are you worried about me all the time?! I'm FINE!" she insisted. "I read my books and watch my shows and call my friends and I can buy whatever I want at the supermarket now without your grandfather yelling at me. So, tonight I'm eating salmon!"

There you have it, ladies. After six-and-a-half decades of always having someone "there," my grandma perfected the art of being alone and avoiding loneliness in just a matter of weeks. She found her outlet—the books and the TV and the phone calls—and a positive perspective on being alone. If she can do that at ninety years of age, I'm damn sure you can do it too.

Stop focusing on the "what if" and focus on the "what is."
What if I never remarry? What if I never have a date to another family function? What if my kids grow up and move across the country and never come visit me? What if? What if? What if?!?!?

Mama, stop. Breathe. Focus. We have no control over what life will be like years from now, let alone minutes from now. One of the best tricks my therapist taught me was to replace the what ifs with what is. Like this:

What if: I never remarry or find another partner?

What is: You have the power to decide if you want to welcome another love into your life. You may not have it yet, but you can certainly work toward finding one.

What if: I never have a date to another family function?

What is: You're not at a family function right now, so why worry about it? Plus, this means you get to escape the awkward questions your family will no doubt lob your date's way once you do have one.

What if: My kids move across the country when they're grown and never visit me?

What is: They're in the next room making a mess of their toys and probably spilling their Goldfish. Cross that bridge when you get there.

Do you see what I'm doing here? I'm trying to talk you off a ledge that hasn't even been built yet. It's harder to feel lonely if you don't spend all your time convincing yourself that you might one day be lonely. Fill your time by enjoying your alone moments instead, so that in case you do have to attend the next few years of family functions on your own, you'll know how to have a badass time with yourself—as you sneak cake into your purse to enjoy alone in bed when you get home.

LONG STORY SHORT

+ *Alone* and *lonely* are two very different words with two very different meanings.

+ If you learn to enjoy being alone, you'll hardly ever feel lonely.

+ Comparison is self-sabotage—stop torturing yourself with it!

+ Find an outlet—like a hobby—for your alone time.

+ Stop what-if-ing and focus on what is.

JOURNAL PROMPT

Write about the things you enjoy doing alone. Use this as a reminder next time you're feeling fearful of having time alone.

CHAPTER 23

Breaking the News of New Love: How to Handle It with Your Ex and Kids

I remember the moment, in the early days of dating Spencer, when I knew this relationship was here to stay. Well, if I'm being honest, I knew right away—as soon as I walked into the lobby of his apartment building to meet him before our first date. As we sat side by side in the back of the Uber on the way to our first dinner. As soon as he kissed me, somewhere between dinner and our next cocktail. Nonetheless, there was a moment just three weeks after our first date that completely validated the feeling I had in my gut of *Holy shit, he's the one.*

It was a steamy Sunday afternoon in May, and we had taken a weekend road trip down to Key West. We had a wonderful time together, but we made the mistake of deciding to drive back up to Miami in holiday weekend traffic, turning a four-hour trip into an eight-hour epic. We crept through traffic, windows down, music on, talking. We talked more on that drive than I felt I had talked to anyone ever in my life, and it was the best talking I had ever done. We shared intimate, personal stories. We shared our fears and insecurities. We shared memories. We shared goals and wants and needs. And I knew after this car ride that I'd be talking to him forever, with such a sense of security, with no judgment, with understanding and compassion.

At the same time, deep inside me, a fire started to rage. A fire fueled by fear that one day I was going to have to tell my ex that I had met someone new. I *dreaded* that conversation, and that dread hung over me all the early days of the relationship. I'd wake up each morning to sweet good-morning texts from my new beloved, before collapsing under the anxiety of having to talk to my ex about it.

I eventually ripped off that Band-Aid, with bile rising in my throat and my heart racing out of my chest, and now, years later, I help other women do the same thing. Only, I help them to do it without shaking like a leaf, weak in the knees, and swallowing tears, like I had done when I had this conversation with my ex at a very inopportune time—while Bella watched a cartoon in the next room and he and I chatted in my kitchen. Ultimately, it's a difficult conversation to have, but inevitable if you do happen to find "the one," or even just the one you plan on spending a lot of time with from here on out. It's only natural that you'll worry about what your ex might think or how he'll react. You'll wonder what he needs to know and how to tell him. You'll worry about the kids—what to tell *them* and how *they'll* take it. Oh, and by the way, when in the hell are you supposed to introduce them? Dating as a co-parent definitely involves a little extra level of stickiness, at first, but here are some ways to make it as smooth as possible.

THE NEED-TO-KNOW BASIS

"Do I need to tell my ex I'm dating again?" many clients have asked me. NO. Hard no. He isn't your friend, your therapist, or your mom. You don't need to tell your ex you're dating again. Even in the most amicable of co-parenting relationships, I've seen shit go south, *fast*, after a client thinks she and her ex are in enough of a "good place" for this level of openness. Old wounds reopen, egos get bruised, and then you're left standing there scratching your head and wondering why in the hell you ever thought it was a good idea to share such personal information with a man you once shared a life with. Don't do it. Your ex-spouse should be kept on a need-to-know basis about your personal life at this point. If things are heating up and getting serious enough where cohabitation or an engagement is looming, that's when he needs to know.

This need-to-know basis extends to your kids too. If you're going on dates—dinner, drinks—there's no need to tell them any details about the people you're meeting. Your children shouldn't have access to your personal life in this way until they absolutely need to—until you're ready to introduce them to your new partner.

SPEAKING OF INTRODUCING THE KIDS . . .

When in hell are you supposed to do that? Well, research and magazine articles and many divorce experts will tell you to wait. And yes, in some ways, waiting is good. You don't want to go ahead and start introducing your children to every single person you meet for dinner or drinks. Introducing the kids too early can cause them confusion about the nature of intimacy, or anxiety over so much change. I agree wholeheartedly with all of this, but here's where my opinion challenges the common "wait" wisdom.

Because of my commitment to motherhood and the fact that I was never going to let a man into my life who didn't intend to love my child, treat her well, and understand that my daughter would always come first, I introduced Bella to Spencer as soon as that "knowing" took over my body. As soon as I knew he'd be a fixture in my life for the foreseeable future, but before there was a ring on my finger. I wanted to see if he was as good a match for her as he was for me. That was important to me. I wanted to see how he would handle her two-year-old needy sweetness, tantrums, and everything in between. I wanted to know that if she threw a juice box across the room, leaving a splotch of apple juice on his West Elm rug, he wouldn't decide I wasn't worth dating. I wanted to know that he could manage the trials and tribulations of parenting right along with me, before I got deeper into a love I wouldn't want to leave.

So, here's what I advise my clients to do:

Wait until you're as sure as you can be that it's real.

Like with your ex, you don't want to rock anyone's world with this new truth if it isn't necessary to do so. You'll know when it's real enough to share the news with your children. Granted, there are no guarantees in life and there's no way to know that this relationship will, indeed, last forever, but use your best mommy judgment here. If he's going to be around for a while and he feels like a safe person to have around your children, then have that conversation.

Make the conversation age-appropriate for your kids.

I didn't introduce Spencer to Bella as the man who had stolen my heart and who I couldn't wait to be with forever. She was two. I introduced him as Mommy's friend, because at that age, the only relationships she understood were the ones with Mommy, Daddy, Gigi, Papa, and the toddlers she toddled with at preschool. The older the child, the clearer you'll need to be about who this person is to you. Your description can go from "Mommy's friend" to "someone Mommy enjoys spending time with" to "someone Mommy loves," depending on your children's level of understanding.

Understand that your kids may feel threatened.

A two-year-old? Not so much. But the older the children, the more they may worry that this new person in your life will take you away from them and divide your attention. Make sure you explain to your kids that this new love interest isn't there to take away from anything, will never come before your love for them, and will never stop you from giving them all the mommy attention they crave from you.

Do NOT go from zero to sixty overnight.

So, you've introduced your new partner to your kids and things went smoothly? Great. Ready to start blending your families and make this an everyday thing? Not so fast. Your children need time to process this relationship even if they display positive feelings toward it. If your new love interest is suddenly all up in your plans with the kids every single day, this could lead to resentment—and you don't want that! Because this happened to me as a child, I knew that I did not want the same for my daughter or Spencer's. His daughter was just ten when we met, and harboring more feelings about her parents' split than mine was, so I made it a point to tread lightly—*very* lightly. The first meeting took place informally, casually, and with both our girls for an early dinner in a busy part of town. The girls took to each other immediately, even after Bella and her two-year-old reflexes sent a full glass of water cascading down the table and onto the floor. It was refreshing to have crossed this bridge, and even though it was a really big deal for us, it felt simple, sweet, and effortless. After this, Spencer would invite us to join them almost every time they were together, but I'd say no a lot, and encourage him to give his daughter the alone time she needed with her daddy. It was as if I wanted to right the wrongs of my own father through their relationship, protecting her little heart to make up for how mine was stomped on. I waited until she started asking that I join them for breakfasts or dinners before I made myself more of a constant presence. I never wanted her to feel as threatened by me as I once did by my father's girlfriend. As for Bella, she rarely saw Spencer around for the first few months. She knew he existed, but knew that Mommy was hers first.

Just because your relationship feels like a fairy tale, don't expect the kids to feel the same.
There's no telling when, or if, your children will take to your new paramour with the same love-at-first-sight gusto that you did. Don't expect it and don't try to force it. The more you push for the relationship to feel like a fairy tale, the less you'll enjoy the process—and the more you'll disappoint yourself. It may take months, if not years, for your kids to warm up in the way you want them to, but don't worry—it all has a way of working out.

Don't worry about what your ex will say.
If you're living *la vida* co-parenting with a high-conflict ex, he's bound to harbor some pretty nasty feelings toward your

new relationship. I worked with a client once whose ex had added all sorts of insane clauses to their parenting plan, including when and how her children could meet her new partner. He demanded to know the activities the kids would be partaking in with this new person and then used the information to badger my client and her children. He eventually became so hostile toward the idea that she'd moved on that he took her to court, where he asked the judge to ban her friend from being around the children, claiming that she was a bad mother for bringing this man around and that he wasn't okay with her choices. The judge told him to stop wasting his time and to get over it.

Chances are, your ex might not have much positivity to share toward you and your new relationship. Repeat after me:

I'm no longer married to this person, and I deserve to feel loved again.

I am worthy of love, and my children will benefit from seeing their mother be respected and treated like the queen she is.

If my ex should talk negatively about my relationship or my new partner to my children, he's doing damage that he will have to live with and that my children will resent him for.

I feel very strongly about these issues. I lived them as a child, under the care of a parent who was vile toward the other, and they're tough to navigate. If your child comes home and says that their father is talking badly about this new person in your life, the best way to handle it is by asking your child how they feel about this person, reminding them that they're allowed to have their own opinions separate from Mommy's or Daddy's, and that Daddy doesn't know this person well enough to like him or not.

Remind yourself of what *you* deserve.

Like I said above, you are worthy of love. If you have found it again, embrace it, cherish it, and don't let it go simply because your ex feels hurt or threatened by it. This is YOUR life, your heart, your story. Your ex might try to make this new relationship difficult for you, but don't let that take away from your beautiful new experience. You worked hard to get here.

LONG STORY SHORT

+ Keep your ex on a need-to-know basis.

+ Use your judgment about when the right time is to introduce your kids to your new love interest.

+ Use age-appropriate ways to discuss this new relationship with your child.

+ Constantly reassure your kids of your love for them and their importance in your life, no matter how well they seem to take to this new person.

+ Don't go from introducing the kids to spending all your time together. Let it evolve naturally.

+ Don't expect fairy tales. This is real life, not Disney.

+ Don't worry about how your ex might feel. You deserve all the love and more.

JOURNAL PROMPT

Remind yourself why you deserve love, the best kind, even if it causes a bit of drama with your ex.

CHAPTER 24

Your Happily-Ever-After

I remember the very first time I watched *Eat, Pray, Love* in the movie theater. It was a sweltering day in August when a good friend and I found ourselves in need of a strong dose of female inspiration, as we were both healing from our latest train-wreck relationships. I remember settling into my seat in the refreshingly air-conditioned theater, feeling moved before the movie even started. I remember the chills I felt as Julia Roberts's character lay broken on the bedroom floor. I remember how giddy I felt when she first landed in Italy, my favorite place, and began to rediscover herself—and carbs. I remember the envy I felt for her when her two Italian travel buddies became engaged, leaving her to continue in search of her happiness alone. I remember wanting to pack up my life into a suitcase, hop on the next plane to Bali, and find my own Javier Bardem to woo me back to life.

I saw it twice more in the theater, then read the book cover to cover, and quickly became obsessed with all things Elizabeth Gilbert. I was so inspired by Liz's undying commitment to finding her version of "happily ever after."

CREATE YOUR OWN VERSION OF HAPPY

I wanted to be one of those Liz Gilbert–types of women so badly. I wanted to say "fuck it!," not worry about what anyone thought, and just *go*. But I was only in my mid-twenties when the movie first rocked my world, with no hint of a husband or divorce in sight, at the very beginnings of a teaching career. It wasn't my time to pack up everything I owned into a suitcase and fly halfway around the world in pursuit of pasta, prayer, and passion—in pursuit of true pleasure. Or at least, I didn't think it was. But that didn't mean I couldn't dream about it.

Fast-forward about seven years, and there I was once again, lying in bed post-separation, watching *Eat, Pray, Love* for the thousandth time. With a two-year-old asleep in the next room, I still wasn't catching that plane to Bali. But that didn't mean I couldn't set out in pursuit of my own happily-ever-after—which meant giving myself the time to flourish and grow and find my self-confidence again. And the same goes for you.

After a divorce, especially if you're relatively young, you're bound to be questioned about your plans for remarriage. I was, by just about everyone I knew, and some folks I didn't. They weren't sure what else to expect of a young woman besides (more) marriage, which is an unfortunate failure of imagination. There's no rule in the world that says your fairy tale can only be written with a partner or spouse by your side, but unfortunately, we women have been programmed throughout our lives—through Disney stories, romantic comedies, covers of magazines, and just about everything else—to believe that marriage should be the primary goal, the thing to save us. "Find your dream man in three simple steps!" "How to be more attractive to get a man!" "Get married or die!" Okay, maybe that last one was a bit dramatic, but you get where I'm going here. Marriage isn't the thing that will save you. No, no, no. Chase pasta. Chase passion. Chase whatever it is your heart desires *first*, and maybe love will settle back into your life once you've got your own story written right.

YOU will save you.

Now, I know I'm remarried and all that, happy as hell to have found my forever Javier Bardem—but I no longer believe that marriage should be the ultimate happily-ever-after goal of anyone's life, especially after a divorce. Marriage—before or after divorce—should be a bonus, in my humble opinion. It should be a special addition to the life you've already fallen in love with. The life you've created just for you, after getting to know every inch of yourself, the good and the bad. It should be a piece of your wildly complex puzzle, the piece you accidentally find under the couch years after you begin to put your puzzle together, that ends up fitting seamlessly into the larger picture of your life. I don't believe marriage should be the whole picture, your whole purpose, or the thing you build your life around. I found my puzzle piece after doing the work, after committing to my own happiness—alone—first.

My happily-ever-after occurred when I finally gave myself permission to fall in love with who I am—a resilient, forward-moving mama—after years of self-loathing, self-sabotaging, and self-doubt. It came when I gave up the idea of what I thought I *should* be doing and began doing the things I *wanted* to do. It came when I finally committed to healing and growing, clawing my way out of the remnants of my childhood that had left me feeling emotionally paralyzed. My happily-ever-after was so much better for not being centered around one person or relationship. It was about putting ME at the center, making myself happy, and enjoying what came as a result of that so I could show up as my best self, day in and day out, for Bella and me. I know with every fiber of my being that I could not be in the marriage I'm in today, one that feels entirely designed for me, had I not changed my perspective on what happily-ever-after truly meant to me.

Now is the time you need to ask yourself whether you're going to put your future happiness in the hands of another partner, or if you're going to make yourself happy and leave the rest up to the universe. This time in your journey—after heartbreak and setbacks and painful growth—is exactly when you're poised to realize that, with a future full of opportunities, possibilities, and your newfound ability to create a life you love, there's so much more that can bring a wholeness and completion to your story. Marriage is a truly wonderful part of my big picture, don't get me wrong, but it isn't my *whole* existence, like I once thought it was supposed to be.

If you feel the pressure to remarry, take it as nothing new. We all felt the pressure to settle down and get married the first time, right? If you don't feel truly ready to commit yourself to someone else, don't do that yet. Do *you* instead. Figure out what your happily-ever-after looks like. Owning it is something you owe yourself—and something you'll never regret doing. The second you tie your happiness to another person, you give that person the power to take that happiness away and set yourself up for overwhelming disappointment when there's a disagreement or betrayal. You need to get to a place where, if you end up in the best relationship in the world and things take a turn for the worse, you'll be left with a few less droplets of happiness, not an entirely empty glass. So, how do you quiet the noise around you that's filled with the "shoulds" and focus on what you truly want?

You may think that your ultimate happiness can be found inside the walls of that red-brick colonial home, tucked inside the white picket fence that surrounds it, or in the depths of that expensive handbag your husband gifted you for your birthday. But that's not always the case. Accept that your truest and deepest needs may be far different from what you originally thought you wanted. That they may be found in feelings instead. And there's absolutely nothing wrong with that.

> Happiness is the consequence of personal effort. You fight for it, strive for it, insist upon it, and sometimes even travel around the world looking for it. You have to participate relentlessly in the manifestations of your own blessings. And once you have achieved a state of happiness, you must never become lax about maintaining it. You must make a mighty effort to keep swimming upward into that happiness forever, to stay afloat on top of it.
>
> —Elizabeth Gilbert, *Eat, Pray, Love*

GO AFTER THAT THING YOU CAN'T STOP THINKING ABOUT

I was so bogged down emotionally and physically by the heaviness of my marriage that all my fantasies revolved around a day when I could wake up in my own home with Bella, surrounded by love, light, and girl-power décor. Every last one of my thoughts revolved around being able to give Bella and me a home without tension and fighting and replace it with sheer happiness, good vibes, and positive energy. Every morning after dropping Bella off at preschool, I would pass by a little townhome community in the city I set my sights on and dream of moving just the two of us into one of those homes.

That was the first thing I did when my marriage imploded. I moved Bella and me into the home I'd dreamed of. I was so enchanted with creating a new life for us there that felt so much better than the last one. I truly remember feeling like life couldn't get any better than finally having our own happy place. In my mind, I would wake up each morning feeling exactly how I wanted to feel in our peaceful little nest for two. Allowing myself to envision such a life helped give me the courage I needed to see my divorce not as an end, but as a beginning. Even now, in my big, beautiful home with my big, beautiful blended family, I have immense love for that small home in my heart because I know that if that was the last place we ever lived, it would have been so much more than enough for me.

I implore you to think about where you want to be physically and how you want it to feel. Write about it in your journal. Draw a picture of it. Imagine it as if there were no other place to be, as if it were just going to be you and your kids and no one else forever. What would this place look like? What would the energy feel like? How would it add value and happiness to your life if you gave yourself permission to feel happiness for yourself and your kids?

THINK OUTSIDE THE BOX

Somewhere in the middle of my first marriage, I gave up my safe teaching career and took a risk. I decided to become a writer, thus committing myself to a life of financial uncertainty. I quickly learned that freelance articles would not pay the rent, so

I pivoted. From the foundation I laid with my passion for writing, I built a marketing company that allowed me to write for other people's websites and business blogs.

Somewhere in the beginning of my split, my family urged me to go back to teaching, where I'd have safety and security. They were concerned, but my determination far outweighed their worry. "No way," I remember telling them. "Not happening." I was gaining so much fulfillment from following my passion that the last thing I wanted to do while my world was upending was give it all up. While running and growing my own business as a single mom was tough, I never gave up, because I've always known that my true passion is—and always will be—writing and helping others through my words. And it turned out to be the right decision.

I think it's critically important that, as your life takes a turn into the world of divorce, you steadfastly commit yourself to a job—or at least a hobby if you don't need to or choose not to have a job outside the work of motherhood—that brings you endless pleasure. My work has been the single most fulfilling and satisfying part of my life (after raising Bella, of course), and you can imagine how elated I felt doing all of my writing in my new little good-vibes town house. My cup overflowed and I felt full of light—lighter than I had been in years—especially knowing that I was solely responsible for my happiness.

LONG STORY SHORT

✦ Happiness is an inside job.

✦ Your happily-ever-after shouldn't be tied to another person; let that other person be a bonus.

✦ Listen to your own needs first in order to find out what makes you truly happy.

✦ Find the happiness in feelings and experiences more than things.

JOURNAL PROMPT

Write about what your happily-ever-after looks like in your mind. Not what you think it's supposed to look like, what you truly want it to be.

CHAPTER 25

All at Once or Nothing at All: The Full Reinvention

The concept of reinvention was once described as "the purest form of hope" by author Phil Wohl. Reinvention means evolving—the way all living beings do, but in a conscious and deliberate way.[1] Reinvention is the thing that happens when a slate is wiped clean and a new story is ready to be written. It's the opportunity one grabs with both hands when there's nowhere left to go but up. Reinvention is the process of life that I'm most obsessed with; it's what has taken me from rock bottom to rocking life more times than I can count.

GIVE YOURSELF PERMISSION TO BECOME ENTIRELY NEW

"I feel like everything is happening at once. Is it too much?" a friend asked me, on the same call in which she shared that she had officially filed for divorce. "I'm moving to a new apartment in the city this summer. My internship is coming to an end, and I'm applying for jobs. My daughter is going to start school in a few months. I just joined a new tennis league. Am I crazy to do all of this at the same time?"

"Not crazy," I said. "You're doing what every woman on God's green Earth should only be so lucky to have the opportunity to do at least once in her life. You're reinventing yourself. You're becoming entirely new."

Very often, in times of relationship transition, women will get the urge to make changes that help free them of anything and everything that holds a reminder of what once was. This desire to change may come on suddenly, dramatically, and go from a want to a need in seconds. Because reinventing yourself often means untying yourself from what you felt has held you back. It means letting go of things that may have felt safe but were actually serving no purpose in your life at all. It's not uncommon to meet a woman who finally found the guts to do something—anything—she had been holding back from doing because her marriage made her feel she had to conform in some way, shape, or form. For some, it's something physical, like a drastic new haircut—a common post-divorce move. It was Coco Chanel who once said that "a woman who cuts her hair is about to change her life." Renee Engeln, a psychology professor and author of *Beauty Sick: How the Cultural Obsession with Appearance Hurts Girls and Women*, has clarified this statement by adding that "making a radical change to your appearance can be a way of sending the message that you're also making a radical change to your life—or that you'd like to." Think of hair as just a metaphor here.

One woman's drastically different new hairstyle may be another woman's "Screw it, I'm pulling a Liz Gilbert and moving to Bali." Or she might sign up for lessons in a new sport she's been dying to learn. Another woman might finally work up the courage to apply for that higher-paying job within her company, because what does she have to lose? Another might paint her bedroom wall a strong, feminine color, or pierce a part of her body that once felt naughty or inappropriate. She might even do all of the above. Freedom has a million ways of manifesting.

For me, it was about so much more than my hair. Making both physical *and* emotional changes after my split was my way of saying, "I'm back, baby, and this time I'm doing things *my* way."

What I'm saying here is that divorce *can* be inspiring. In fact, I surveyed a group of my past clients, and almost all of them admitted to applying for new jobs with higher salaries after their divorces. "I simply wanted to change my job just because my ex insisted I could never do better," one client shared. Another told me that her boss started to feel as controlling as her ex, belittling her when she dared to ask a question, so she leveled up just to throw it in both their faces. Whether the changes you want to make are personal, a proverbial middle finger to your ex, or both, they're bound to feel damn good.

"Are there any changes that are off limits?" I've been asked. I think that depends on one's own sense of risk, to be honest. So long as it doesn't hurt you or your children, why not go for it? Why not throw caution to the wind and do the things you dreamed of doing—but couldn't do—in your marriage? This isn't necessarily rhetorical. The reason we get this sudden urge to grab life by the balls and turn it upside down, but stop ourselves dead in our tracks, is usually fear: fear of the unknown, fear of shaking things up, and fear of what people might say.

PUT ON YOUR BLINDERS
AND IGNORE THE NAYSAYERS

The one problem with making changes to your life after a divorce is that it can make the people around you slightly uncomfortable. Your ex will balk at your post-divorce choices. Your in-laws? They'll swear you've entered an early midlife crisis. But they're bound to judge no matter what, so let's ignore them for a second. It's the people close to you, the ones who are *supposed* to be in your camp no matter what, who may feel a little put off by your changes, leaving you to wonder whether you're making the right decisions or not. They'll tell you in a way that doesn't sound encouraging that they notice how you've changed. They, too, might wonder if you've lost your mind.

I have news for you: that's their problem, not yours. You cannot let people talk fear into your plans. It's okay to ask them to step aside as you charge forth.

I know whereof I speak. When I started taking risks, as a budding entrepreneur in the early stages of my divorce, my family actually staged a what-is-wrong-with-you–style *intervention*. My mom and brother showed up at my door on a rainy Saturday afternoon, claiming to want to visit Bella, but smuggling in a secret agenda.

"Michelle, come sit with us a second," my brother said from the living room, as I felt the room close in on me. "We just can't help but think that this move you're making to leave your career is absolutely crazy," he pleaded.

"You'll never make money as a writer, and you're dreaming if you think you will," my mom chimed in.

I was defensive, I was annoyed, but I also knew deep down inside that eventually, I'd prove them wrong. They didn't know what I felt in my gut. They also didn't have to live with my choices; I did. The choices you make as you harness the power of reinvention after divorce may not make much sense to people who aren't living your life. They may be thinking, "I could never do this, so why can you?" But that's exactly it. Their perspective and yours are totally different. Someone who isn't in your shoes, playing by the same rules, shouldn't have the ability to coach your game. They shouldn't even have the option to comment from the sidelines. This is your Super Bowl now, your mega, life-defining moment. So, where are you going next? What's it going to be? New hair or a new country code? Whichever you choose, make sure it's something that truly makes you feel alive and helps you set yourself apart from the life you just ended.

If you're ready for your reinvention, here's how I suggest you go about taking some new, big, beautiful leaps into evolving higher.

TAKING THE FIRST STEP
INTO SOMETHING NEW

I'm a huge fan of new beginnings. I love a fresh start, a renewed lease on life, and utilizing both to my full potential. I up and left New York within a week of deciding to move to Miami in search of a new life. I quit a teaching career I'd spent years studying for and working in to declare myself a writer and a budding entrepreneur. I separated from a marriage after only three years, following my gut and trusting in my ability to start anew on my own. I made all the changes I felt compelled to make: moving to a new house, getting back in the gym, and while not cutting my hair, throwing some lighter highlights in it. A full reinvention, in my opinion, is another way of saying, "I have one life and one life only, and I intend to use it well." But how do you make that leap? How do you bridge the gap from the here and now to the great unknown, into wanting more, better, bigger?

It all starts with taking the first step and understanding that there is literally nothing holding you back from being the kind of woman, mom, and life disruptor you're dying to be.

LET GO OF SHAME

There's no shame in you doing you, though those closest to you and the rest of the peanut gallery may think there is as they pepper your plans with their opinions. Pay this chatter no mind. This is about your life, no one else's. People can see things only through the lens of the life they're living. There's no shame in wanting to shed the skin of a life that brought you pain so you can step into a brand-new one. There's no shame in craving your own version of happiness. There's no shame in having hope that a certain level of change will catapult you into a more evolved version of yourself, making you the best mom, woman, and human you can possibly be—because that's exactly what happens when you take that leap.

GET CLEAR ON YOUR VERSION OF REINVENTION

It doesn't have to be a Britney Spears 2007 head-shaving moment. You don't need to pull up to school in a shiny red sports car. You don't need to sacrifice your child's college fund and splurge on plastic surgery for bigger or smaller parts. In fact, your reinvention doesn't have to be physically or aesthetically centered at all. Acknowledging the parts of you that need work and healing, vowing to make better choices as you move forward in life, committing to self-care and emotional growth—these are all ways you can reinvent yourself for the better. Or maybe, like I was, you're desperate to reconnect with the values and beliefs in your life you pushed to the side in order to make others happy. So long as it feels good to you, makes sense in your head, and is aligned with the life you want to live after your divorce, your version of reinvention can be whatever it needs to be. Get clear on what you truly want to change, ignore what society thinks or tells you to do, and go for it.

BE HONEST WITH YOURSELF

There's a big difference between running away from your problems and making changes for the better. When you find yourself ready to make changes in how you live your life after a divorce, you also need to ask yourself whether you're about to engage in said change to:

A. Get your ex to notice you

B. Piss off your ex

C. Distract from the pain you need to heal from

D. A & B

E. All of the above

If you answered yes to any of these questions, you need to get honest with yourself about your choices. Do you want this change for you, or for the hope that it'll make him feel more regretful and you less bitter? Do you want this change because you're ready for it or are you delaying the inevitable of doing the work to heal from your past? Ask yourself why you truly want to make these changes, and then be sure that the ones you choose to make have nothing to do with anyone but you.

HARNESS YOUR COURAGE

It's not uncommon to face feelings of fear and self-doubt when boarding the bus to the unknown. Taking risks will push you way outside your comfort zone and will require a level of courage that forces you to believe in yourself, even if the "newness" of your changes doesn't feel all that comfortable yet. Stick it out. Go the distance. Harness the same courage you needed to reach down inside yourself and find the last time you did a hard thing. It's in there, definitely, but sometimes you just need to set an internal alarm clock and wake that baby up.

BE PATIENT: ROME WASN'T BUILT IN A DAY

When you decide to reinvent yourself, you're making the conscious decision to build a better version of the "you" you're used to. But in the process, don't forget that you, my dear, are already a masterpiece. And though you may be making fundamental changes related to the structure of your life, you will need patience. You're dipping your toes into a whole new world, setting the foundation for a whole new life, and learning so much in the process. It won't happen overnight. It won't happen in a week, either, but I can pretty much guarantee that a year from now, you'll be able to look back in awe at everything you've accomplished by sticking to your commitment and taking advantage of this opportunity to evolve in the best way possible.

LONG STORY SHORT

✦ It's okay to want to reinvent your life after divorce.

✦ It's not okay to let anyone talk you out of the decisions you want to make: this is your life and yours alone.

✦ Your reinvention can be as benign as a change in hair color or as major as a move across the world. It's personal and needs to be about you.

✦ A good place to start your reinvention is deep within you.

✦ Get honest with yourself about the changes you want to make.

✦ Be patient—Rome wasn't built in a day.

JOURNAL PROMPT

What do you feel inspired to do now that you're starting this new chapter in your life?

CHAPTER 26

One Step Forward, Three Steps Back

So, here you are. You've spent a solid amount of time getting past this marriage. You've done the work, you've cried the tears, you've felt the feelings, and you've spent more time alone than you ever imagined you could handle. You're stronger now; you feel a revived sense of confidence starting to seep out from your soul ever so slowly, making its way to the corners of your mouth and finally turning them in the right direction whenever you think about the possibilities that lie ahead. You can finally look back and admire how far you've come, reassuring yourself that if you can get through the black hole of hell that is the divorce process, figure out how to live life as a co-parent, and manage single motherhood, you can literally do *anything*.

And then one day, after how far you've come, you wake up overcome with grief, anger coursing through your veins, and completely unable to function. You literally "can't even," and what's worse is that you don't know where all of this is coming from, thrusting you deep into the pits of shame and guilt, and you're utterly disappointed in yourself for feeling this way.

This is so normal. Prepare for it, Mama. You've just journeyed all the way to the moon for the very first time, and it was no doubt a scary ride. You held yourself together for all of it, vowing to do the best you could do as each surprise roadblock presented itself. You've allowed yourself to venture well outside the comforts of what lived within the stratosphere you left behind. You're on new terrain now. Though you've made it in one piece, there are still bound to be days or moments or situations that arise that leave you feeling like you're gasping for air, desperate to run back into the shelter of your spaceship and head toward the life you left behind.

You're allowed to take one giant leap forward into the unknown, and three steps back.

I certainly did. Having spent the better part of my first year sans husband feeling strong, confident, and determined to keep moving forward, I found myself facedown in bed in the middle of a Tuesday, ignoring my work, my appointments, and the carpool line that I should have already been in. I didn't know where this sudden rush of emotions was coming from. My first thought was to wonder whether or not I had forgotten to take my magic pill, the Zoloft that gave me balance, and my second thought was whether or not I was getting my period. Nope, it was neither of those things. It was simple, overwhelming grief, and it wasn't anyone's fault. But it didn't feel great, and I didn't expect to be feeling it again after getting through those first few icky months of separation. I hadn't yet learned about the process of healing. In my mind, it meant you cry, you get over it, you go to therapy, and POOF, you're healed. I didn't know then what I know now: that the process of healing is anything but linear.

FROM SETBACKS TO BACK IN ACTION

Looking back, I now know that those healing setbacks came as a message from the universe to pull me back down to Earth for a moment, as it nudged me gently to remind me that I'm human, after all. Not above feeling pain, not immune to the natural emotional roller coaster we find ourselves on from time to time. It was a reminder that the task I had taken on, as a woman, a mother, and a survivor, was so much bigger than me. Honoring that life has become a lot heavier than I ever anticipated. I now know that these setbacks are a chance to grab hold of your perspective, take a few deep breaths, and spring back into action.

My whole philosophy of moving on has never, for one minute, been based on the idea that you should ignore your emotions or the difficulty of the process. In fact, my philosophy of moving on is all about facing the real, shitty ugliness you need to go through in order to get from point A to point B. It's not your ability to ignore the pain that makes you strong and able to keep moving forward, it's your ability to accept it, honor it, and use it as fuel for your rocket ship into the unknown. It's all part of the process, my dear, and nothing good comes easy—but getting there will be so damn worth it.

Here's how to handle the setback days, so you can get back to action:

Vent.

Self-loathing, party of one. You know all of those friends who keep telling you how strong you are, who marvel at all you manage to accomplish despite your pain, and who constantly remind you that you can call them for anything you need? Now's the time to take them up on their offer and start venting. Very often, I find myself holding back from venting, as the thought of being annoying and needy makes me shudder, but thankfully, I have the kind of friends who will listen without judgment. I've never once regretted picking up the phone, prefacing a phone call with "I'm at the end of my rope," and letting it alllllll out. You feel lighter when you do.

Drop the guilt.
If your child was having an exceptionally hard day and was acting more out of sorts than you're used to, would you shame the child for feeling this way, or would you curl up on the couch with that sweet kiddo and cuddle your little butts off? Exactly. Give yourself that same love and permission to feel. Guilt doesn't serve you well, nor will it ever, and it's the last thing you need right now! Give yourself a little grace, cancel your plans, curl up on the couch with yourself and find some comfort. You deserve it.

Look back.
Sit with yourself for a moment to look back in time. Marvel at all you've survived, fought through, dealt with, and overcome. Don't take yourself back in time and stay there—heavens no. Look behind you to remind yourself of how far you've come, because there's no greater motivation than being able to say, "Damn, I did that. Nobody else. Just me. Let's keep going."

Write, baby, write.
If there were ever a time to whip out your journal and put pen to paper, it would be now, when you feel you're three steps behind where you were yesterday, and when it feels like you'll

never get back to where you were before you woke up today. Write about how it feels, how the feelings are making you feel, and how you'd *rather* be feeling. Write about what may or may not have prompted this emotional upheaval, how you're vowing to honor it, and what you plan on doing to move past it. Put the date on it, give the day a name (That Shitty Tuesday, for example), and revisit this entry whenever you're finding yourself down or in a period of self-doubt. You'll need the reminder.

When all else fails, remember that it takes a storm to bring a rainbow. Diamonds are made under pressure. You cannot live your best and boldest life—appreciating it fully—without experiencing the other side. Better days are coming. Trust the process.

LONG STORY SHORT

+ Healing is not linear, and setbacks are inevitable.

+ Setbacks remind us to take a deep breath so we can get back in action.

+ Vent to your heart's content.

+ Let go of guilt.

+ Write your beautiful butt off.

JOURNAL PROMPT

Follow the prompts in this chapter each time you find yourself having a setback. Lather, rinse, repeat.

Epilogue

My entire world was packed into boxes, yet again, for what felt like the thousandth time in my adult life. Move number ten, to be exact. Piled high to the ceiling were the artifacts Bella and I had acquired over the last two years of our time alone in the little town house we loved so much. Peppa Pig toys, my favorite pots and pans that cooked all our meals, every single one of our belongings crammed into boxes with labels that would make sure they stayed organized upon their arrival at their next destination. This time together, alone in a brand-new phase of our lives, had more meaning than anything else I had experienced. This time, in this house, was where the lessons were learned, the pain was felt, the tears were cried, and the setbacks and stumbles and heartaches all came together to strengthen me, preparing to catapult me into the next season of my life. My second chance.

Or was it?

As the movers began hoisting the pieces of my life that I had so proudly rebuilt into a truck that would travel only four miles east, I looked around with shock and awe. Even though the life that waited for me in the home Spencer and I worked so hard to build would prove to be a beautiful one, I was sad to leave this space. I was excited to go but felt a strange sense of loss. This had been a special place, after all.

This was the space that had made me whole again.

The space that taught me that I could, in fact, be alone, after years of doubting my ability to stand on my own two feet.

The space where I learned to go from surviving to thriving as a single mom.

The space where I toiled away in my dining room, my makeshift office, writing the words that paid all the bills—an accomplishment that empowered me beyond words.

The space where I fell in love with myself again.

The space where I allowed myself to welcome a big new love into my life after suffering so much heartache.

The space where Bella and I threw on music in the afternoons and danced around and let the good energy of our happy little home wash over us. The space devoid of any negativity, disrespect, or discontent.

The space that brought me back to life.

As the last pieces of our lives made it onto the truck, I wondered if maybe this new beginning I was about to embark on *wasn't* the second chance I'd been looking for after all, but something else. Perhaps I had already given *myself* my second chance by learning to live life on my own terms, to lead a life not defined by a marriage or lack thereof. These two years in our town house weren't just a layover on the next stop in my life: *this* was the stop that allowed me to pause, reflect, change, and grow, making me secure and strong enough to move myself forward. Perhaps this new life that awaited me was my gift to myself, my gold medal for achieving my most impressive feat yet:

Becoming the me I always needed to be.

As soon as the movers unloaded of all our stuff, I worked

furiously to set up Bella's room, making sure to keep her favorite dolls on her bed and set up her bookshelf just the way she liked it. She had spent the weekend with her dad, and I wanted her to feel settled as soon as she stepped through the door. I welcomed her into our new home after a full weekend of unpacking and organizing and watched her mop of curly brown hair bopping down the hall behind her as she ran to check out her new room. I couldn't help but feel complete. She was a girl on the go, always ready for what was coming next and never looking back. I loved her for that—and I loved me too.

Because I was a mom, moving on, in all the best ways.

Your Step-by-Step Journaling Blueprint

P utting pen to paper comes as naturally to me as breathing. I've always been a list-maker, a thought-jotter, and the notes section in my iPhone is miles long by this point. Writing has been my mode of therapy since the third grade, when my teacher, Mrs. Winston, declared me a "beautiful and thoughtful writer" and always called on me first to read my journal entries. Excuse the humblebrag. I realize that for the rest of the world, or at least the world that didn't grow up collecting journals and pouring their hearts out into them, this may not come as naturally as it did for me.

Here's the good news: you do not, I repeat, you DO NOT need to be a "good writer" to reap the benefits of journaling. It's not about writing style, or spelling, or grammar. It's not about making any sense. It's about releasing your emotions into a safe space, and letting the moment take you where you need to go in your thought process. Journaling is scientifically proven to help you deal with overwhelming emotions by being a healthy outlet for expressing yourself. Journaling has been found to help reduce stress levels, manage anxiety, and even cope with depression.

The best part (at least for a control freak like me)? Journaling helps you take control of your feelings and improve your mood by:

✦ Helping you put order to your fears and concerns

✦ Giving you a better understanding of your triggers and how to control them as you begin to track any symptoms or feelings as they show up

✦ Providing an opportunity for positive self-talk

✦ Identifying negative thoughts and behaviors

Journaling is like creating a blueprint for yourself, of all you want to overcome, achieve, release, and let go of. It helps you identify and make sense of everything that's going on within you. It's powerful and has changed my life in so many ways.

Here's how to get started:

1. Buy a journal.
Search "cute journals" on Amazon and you're bound to find one that appeals to you. My current journal is pink with cute lemons on it and has inspirational quotes plastered all over it, as if that surprises you at all.

2. Make a commitment.
Like with anything else, you've got to be committed if you want to make a change. Set aside time each day, even if it's

just five or ten minutes, to do some journaling. I've always loved ending my day with a good journal sesh, but if you feel fresher and more open to the idea in the morning, by all means, do it when it works for you.

3. Use guided prompts.

The best prompts are always exactly what you're feeling in that moment, letting your gut be your prompt-decider. In case that doesn't work for you, I've created a whole list of prompts at the end of this chapter to help you get started, and it's fun to revisit them from time to time.

4. Don't edit yourself.

These entries aren't being graded, studied, or seen by anyone else. The harder and faster you write, the less worried you are about the itty-bitty details, the more raw and real your entries will turn out. That's exactly what they need to be: raw and real. My suggestion is to avoid full sentences (sorry, Mrs. Winston) and keep your thoughts and ideas bulleted so they're easier to read back later on.

5. Revisit your thoughts.

Reading old journal entries is extremely eye-opening. You'll find yourself in awe of where you are now versus where you were then, and there's no better motivation for moving forward.

MICHELLE'S FIFTY FAVORITE JOURNAL PROMPTS

1. How am I feeling today?

2. What am I worried about right now?

3. When was the last time I felt truly proud of myself?

4. When was the last time I felt truly fulfilled?

5. What makes a good day?

6. What makes a bad day?

7. How would my family describe me?

8. How would my best friends describe me?

9. How would my kids describe me?

10. What if vs. what is: Separating fears from reality

11. What do I need more of in my life?

12. What do I need to let go of? (fears, toxic energy, toxic relationships)

13. What are some of my limiting beliefs that might be holding me back?

14. What are ten things I'm grateful for today?

15. What are ten positive things about my life?

16. What are five ways that I can go out of my comfort zone this year?

17. What are seven things I'm really good at?

18. Write out fifteen positive affirmations (e.g., I can achieve anything set my mind to).

19. What motivates me to keep going?

20. How would I describe myself to someone who has never met me before?

21. What are three of my life passions? (hobbies/things that set my soul on fire)

22. Who is my biggest inspiration and why?

23. Where will I be in five years?

24. What unhealthy habits do I need to cut out?

25. What five things do I love most about myself?

26. What do I struggle with the most?

27. What are five words that describe me best, and why?

28. How can I add happiness to my daily life?

29. What animal describes me as a person, and why?

30. What do I need to forgive myself for?

31. How can I show myself more love?

32. What am I going to achieve next month?

33. What negative mindsets do I need to let go of?

34. What are fifty things that make me smile?

35. What would I do if I knew I could not fail?

36. What would have made that situation suck less?

37. Would I rather have everything I want handed to me and not appreciate it or work hard and struggle for it so the reward feels greater? Why?

38. What is the best compliment I've ever received?

39. How do I want to be remembered?

40. Which family member really "gets me" and how does that benefit my life?

41. What are some values that I refuse to compromise for anyone else?

42. When was the last time I really freaked out over something, but everything turned out okay?

43. What are my go-to comforts when I'm stressed?

44. What is my favorite song? Why does this song resonate with me so deeply?

45. What is my weirdest, quirkiest quality that I secretly love, and why?

46. If I could switch lives with any celebrity for a day, who would it be, and why?

47. If I could win any award, what would be it, and why?

48. What would my ideal partner value about me?

49. What is my ideal vacation plan?

50. What is one thing I wish I could get better at?

I promise that if you try any one of these prompts, one page will eventually turn into three. Three will turn into five, and you'll have discovered the beautifully powerful rabbit hole of getting your thoughts out quietly and privately. Don't beat yourself up if you can't get to it; rather, use it as a fallback plan to help you cope with your darkest of days. There is nothing I enjoy more.

Happy writing!

Acknowledgments

Barry and Alvy: the best men there ever were. The father figures who stepped in when I needed them most. The ones who are always navigating my journey from up above. Thank you for proving that there are good men in this world and for teaching me to do it "my way."

David: the little big brother I couldn't live without. You're one of those good men too.

Herb: the best bonus dad, papa of all papas, and lover of my mom. Thank you for being you.

Jolie: the stepdaughter I'm lucky to love. Thank you for your warmth and kindness.

Jenny: the aunt who has always treated me like her own child. And bought me my first bra. And makes me laugh until I cry. I told you I'd mention you!

Mrs. Winston: the third-grade teacher at Hewitt Elementary School in RVC who helped me find the beauty in writing and confidence in my abilities. Thank you, wherever you are.

Alyse: the best friend who has put up with me since 1986. Thank you for guiding my writing journey with enthusiasm and for the never-ending conversations we've been having since Albany Court.

Jennie Nash, Susanne Dunlap, and Lianne Scott: the literary all-star team. You ladies are the architects of my writing dreams and the best thing that 2020 could have brought me.

Joelle Delbourgo: the JLo of literary agents. Thank you for giving me a second chance. None of this would have been possible without you.

Simon Element/Simon & Schuster: Thank you for taking a chance on me. I would particularly like to thank cover designer Patrick Sullivan, interior designer Davina Mock-Maniscalco, editors Emily Carleton and Samantha Lubash, managing editor Annie Craig, marketing specialist Laura Flavin, production editor Benjamin Holmes, production manager Allison Har-zvi, and publicity specialist Nan Rittenhouse.

Evelyn Mendal, LMHC: the great friend and amazing early childhood expert who shared her knowledge with us in this book. Look how far we've come, Mama!

Sheva Ganz: the friend, therapist, and single-mom coach who was brave enough to share part of her courageous story with us in this book.

My clients, readers, and followers: the women who inspire me more than they know. Each and every one of you has touched my heart, and I'm so grateful for your trust and support.

Liz Gilbert, Brené Brown, Candace Bushnell, Ernest Hemingway, Glennon Doyle: the writers who have inspired me in ways I could never put into words.

Nanny: the best grandma that ever lived. You're my favorite phone date, cheerleader, and friend. Thank you for shaping my life the way that you have.

My husband: We did it. We always do it. You know you crush me. I love you.

My mom: There would be no moving on without you. Thank you for paving the way with such grace, class, elegance, and strength.

Bella: You are my reason, my light, and my proudest accomplishment. Never forget your strength and just how beautiful you are, inside and out. You CAN do anything you set your mind to. I love you the most.

Notes

CHAPTER 1: PULLING YOURSELF OUT OF BED AFTER REALITY SETS IN

1. The Bronfenbrenner Center for Translational Research, "Reduce Stress and Anxiety Levels with Journaling," *Psychology Today*, April 22, 2020, https://www.psychology today.com/us/blog/evidence-based-living/202004 /reduce-stress-and-anxiety-levels-journaling.

CHAPTER 2: THE FIVE W'S OF BREAKING THE NEWS (WHO, WHAT, WHEN, WHERE, WHY, AND HOW TO SPILL THE DIVORCE BEANS)

1. Dona Matthews, PhD, "Should You Stay Together Only for the Kids?" *Psychology Today*, May 29, 2019, https:// www.psychologytoday.com/us/blog/going-beyond -intelligence/201905/should-you-stay-together-only-the -kids.

CHAPTER 3: UNCOMFORTABLE COMFORT: DIS-MANTLING A FAMILY AND LIFE AS YOU KNEW IT

1. Samantha Shanley, "How Do You Keep a Family Together after a Divorce?" *Washington Post*, June 6, 2017, https://www.washingtonpost.com/news/soloish/wp/2017/06/06/how-do-you-keep-a-family-together-after-a-divorce/.

CHAPTER 4: GETTING LAID AFTER DIVORCE, PART 1

1. Lacey Johnson, "The Best Tips for Reinventing Your Sex Life After Divorce," Oprah Daily, March 27, 2020, https://www.oprahmag.com/life/relationships-love/a31956827/sex-after-divorce/.

CHAPTER 7: SURVIVING THE FIRST WEEKEND WITHOUT YOUR KIDS

1. Tara Parker-Pope, "Maternal Instinct Is Wired into the Brain," *New York Times*, March 7, 2008, https://well.blogs.nytimes.com/2008/03/07/maternal-instinct-is-wired-into-the-brain/.

CHAPTER 8: PARENTING IN PIECES: SURVIVING YOUR TIME WITHOUT THE KIDS FROM NOW ON

1. Timothy Grall, "Custodial Mothers and Fathers and Their Child Support: 2013," United States Census Bureau,

January   2016,   https://www.census.gov/content/dam
/Census/library/publications/2016/demo/P60-255.pdf.

2. Bari Walsh, "The Science of Resilience," Harvard Graduate
School of Education, March 23, 2015, https://www.gse
.harvard.edu/news/uk/15/03/science-resilience.

CHAPTER 9: SPEAKING OF KIDS, THEY'RE RUINED FOREVER, RIGHT? HOW KIDS PROCESS DIVORCE AT EVERY AGE

1. Carl E. Pickhardt, PhD, "How Parental Divorce Can
Impact Adolescence Now and Later," *Psychology Today*,
November 2, 2015, https://www.psychologytoday.com
/us/blog/surviving-your-childs-adolescence/201511
/how-parental-divorce-can-impact-adolescence-now-and.

2. Neil Farber, MD, PhD, CLC, CPT, "Enhancing Positive
Outcomes for Children of Divorce," *Psychology Today*,
March 30, 2018, https://www.psychologytoday.com/ie
/blog/the-blame-game/201803/enhancing-positive
-outcomes-children-divorce.

3. Scott T. Ashby, "Parental Alienation Syndrome: What
It Is and How to Identify It," Pacific Northwest Family
Law, March 13, 2019, https://pnwfamilylaw.com/parental
-alienation-syndrome/#:~:text=Parental%20Alienation
%20often%20occurs%20if,Borderline%20Personality%20
Disorder.

4. Richard A. Gardner, MD, "The Parental Alienation Syndrome: Past, Present, and Future," RichardAGardner .com, October 18, 2002, http://richardagardner.com/ar22.

CHAPTER 13: I HATE MY EX. WILL MY ANGER EVER GO AWAY?

1. Berit Brogaard, DMSci, PhD, "It's a Thin Line between Love and Hate," *Psychology Today*, March 27, 2018, https:// www.psychologytoday.com/us/blog/the-mysteries -love/201803/it-s-thin-line-between-love-and-hate.

CHAPTER 16: GETTING OVER BETRAYAL AND GASLIGHTING, AND LEARNING TO TRUST YOUR GUT AGAIN

1. Roy T. Bennett, *The Light in the Heart: Inspirational Thoughts for Living Your Best Life* (self-published, 2016).

CHAPTER 17: BREAKING OLD PATTERNS AND UNDERSTANDING YOUR ATTACHMENT STYLE

1. Jade Wu, "Which of These Four Attachment Styles Is Yours?" *Scientific American*, June 26, 2020, https://www .scientificamerican.com/article/which-of-these-four -attachment-styles-is-yours/.

CHAPTER 25: ALL AT ONCE OR NOTHING AT ALL: THE FULL REINVENTION

1. Lydia Sweatt, "17 Inspiring Quotes About Reinventing Yourself," *Success*, October 20, 2016, https://www.success .com/17-inspiring-quotes-about-reinventing-yourself/.